We Make the World Magazine
A Literary & Art Magazine Made By and For Young People

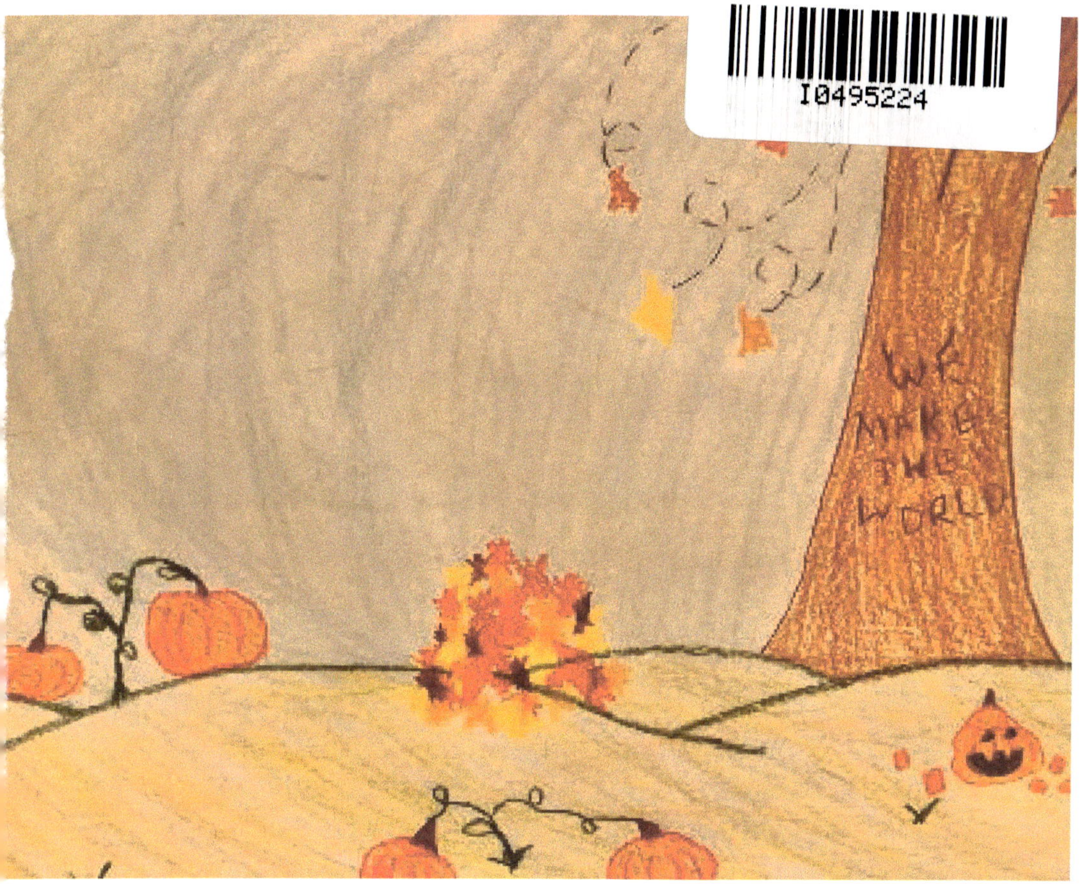

Turning, Changing, Swaying, Falling

FALL 2020

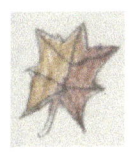
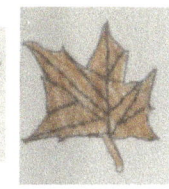
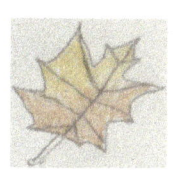
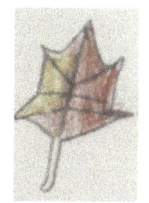

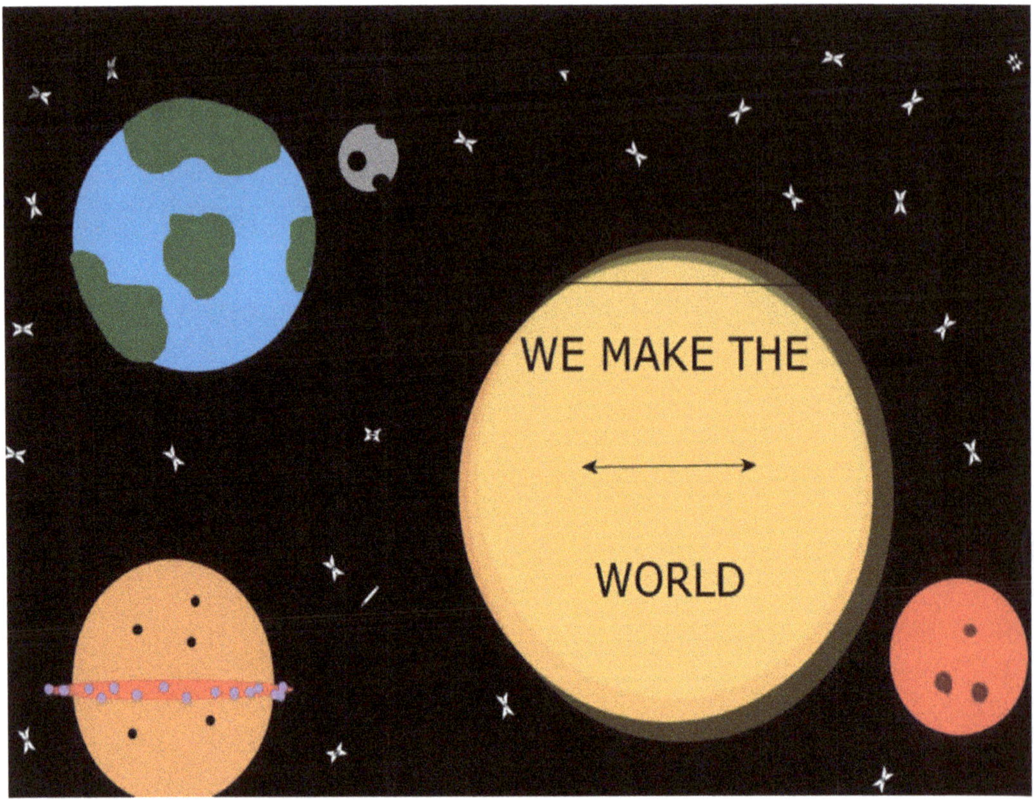

Art by Ava Muhlestein, 11

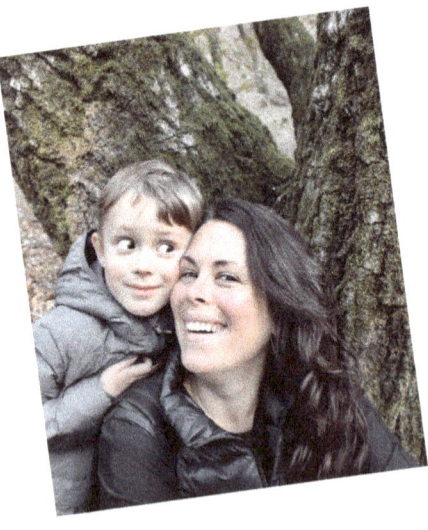

Welcome to the second issue of We Make the World Magazine (WMWM), a creative literary and art magazine made by and for young people!

In our Fall 2020 Issue "Turning, Changing, Swaying, Falling" we explore the season and nature through creative writing, art, puzzles, food and poetry.

WMWM is a seasonal magazine connected to literary and arts based classes where students learn to find their voice and explore what inspires them to create. To order more copies, get an e-magazine, or find out about upcoming classes, contact us at tracyrandolph@hotmail.com to learn more.
Happy reading!

WMWM Director, Tracy Randolph

Cover Art by Luna Rose Randolph, 10

FALL 2020 CONTRIBUTORS

Leila Goldstein, 10
Leila likes to read stories about adventures and write about strange things, she also likes arts & crafts. Her birthday is 8/2/10 and she likes cream cheese frosting on her birthday cakes. Her favorite animals are a fox and a wolf.

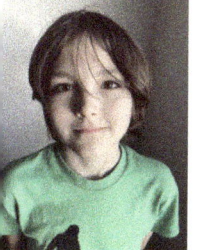

James Clawson, 11
James enjoys reading and writing fantasy and horror, playing video games,(especially Legend of Zelda,) he has an alter ego as a character named Alan Willow, and three of his favorite words are paranormal, dragon, and friendship.

Ava Muhlestein, 11
Ava likes the color purple, she loves to sing, rollerblade, painting, reading, anything science or slime. Ava lives on a ranch that has goats, chickens, rabbits, pigs, dogs, cats and a donkey. She has six siblings and has been attending Tracy's classes for the past three years and she loves it! Her favorite words are SASQUATCH, star clusters, weird, pickles and technically.

Matty Randolph, 13 going on 14
Matty likes and knows everything about Pokemon, Mega Man, and Cuphead. He likes to animate, and writes his own series, Call to a Quest. He likes using the underside of his spoon to eat yogurt, which is unsettling. His favorite words of 2020 are Peridot, irradiated, and crystallized.

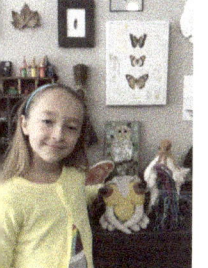

Luna Rose, 10
Luna loves performing in theatre. She loves reading and writing about dragons, fantasy, and romance. Luna also is a number one fan of the Keeper of the Lost Cities books, her favorite words are death, kill, and Groot. (P.S. NEVER mess with her, or else)

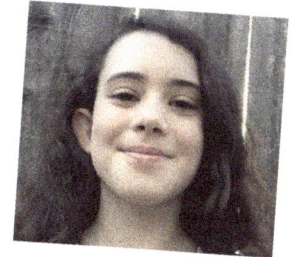

Annika Arvik, 10
Annika loves to read Nancy Drew! She loves to write and read about dragons! Favorite animal: Cuttlefish. Top #3 Favorite words: Thither, officially, Deoxyribonucleic acid.

Crispin Campbell, 11
Crispin likes to write scary stories and fantasy. He likes to read things with magic and wizards. His three favorite words are sorcery, enigma, and xenacanth, which is a kind of extinct shark. He is 11 and likes marine biology, Legos, and cats.

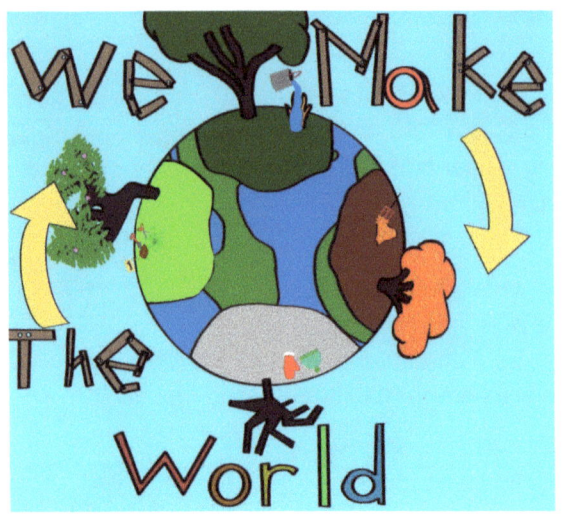

We Make the World!
By: Annika, 10

The world to thee,
We turn ourselves in seeking,
the world has a meaning,
a special meaning,
home, shelter, roof over the skies,
we help the world help us.

World Art by Leila

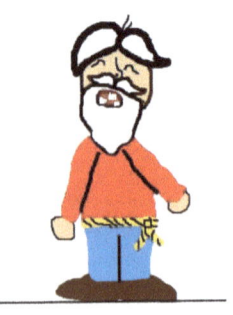

Gnomes by Annika

They gather up in little houses, and they are always kind to deer and mouses. They sleep under mushrooms, oh, how divine! But the gnomes can't sleep in straight lines…

..................................Fall..................................
By Annika

Fall, the leaves are falling.
Fall, the air is crisp.
Fall, the apples are ripe.
Fall, the pumpkins are ready.
Fall, the leaves are crumbling.
Fall, Everyone is asleep?

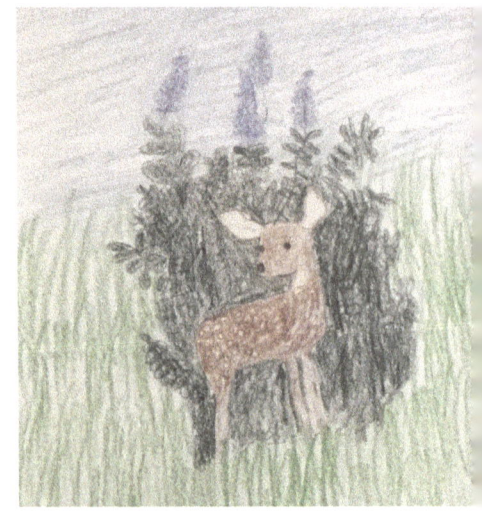

Baby Deer by Leila

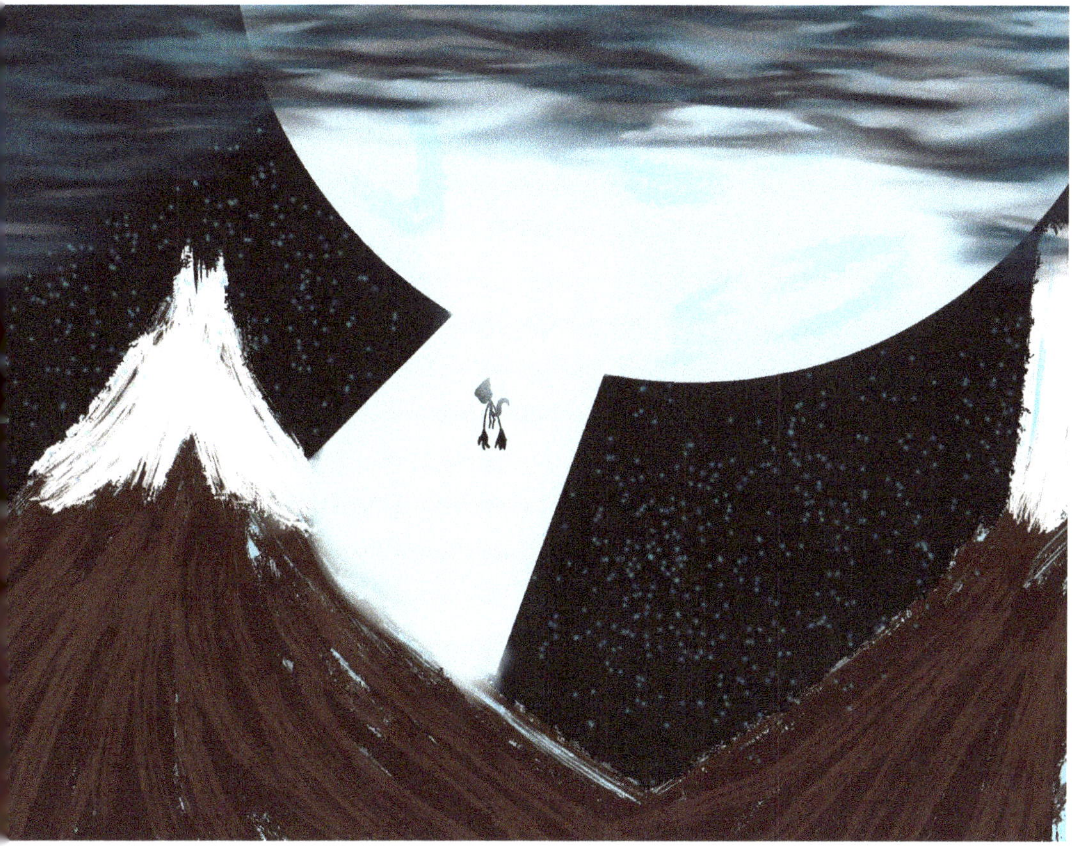

Art by Matty

TRICK OR TREAT
By Annika, 10
You need to trick the treat to get the trick.
To go treating, you need to treat the trick, to trick the treat.
To spend the night tricking, you need to give the trick a treat, so that the trick will get the treat and trick.
The treat and the trick, trick the treat to get the trick.
To treat, treat the trick to get the treat.

Trick or Treat Art by James

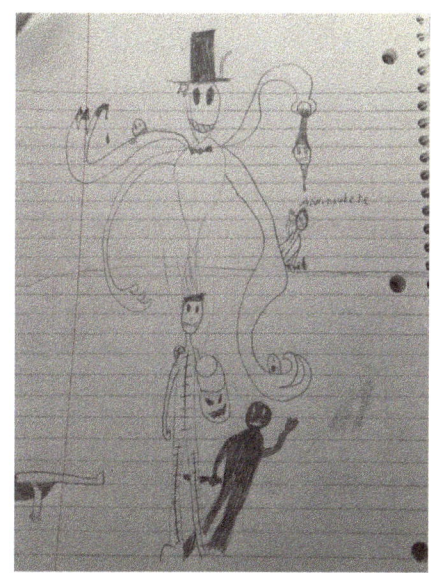

Maze!

By: Leila Goldstein

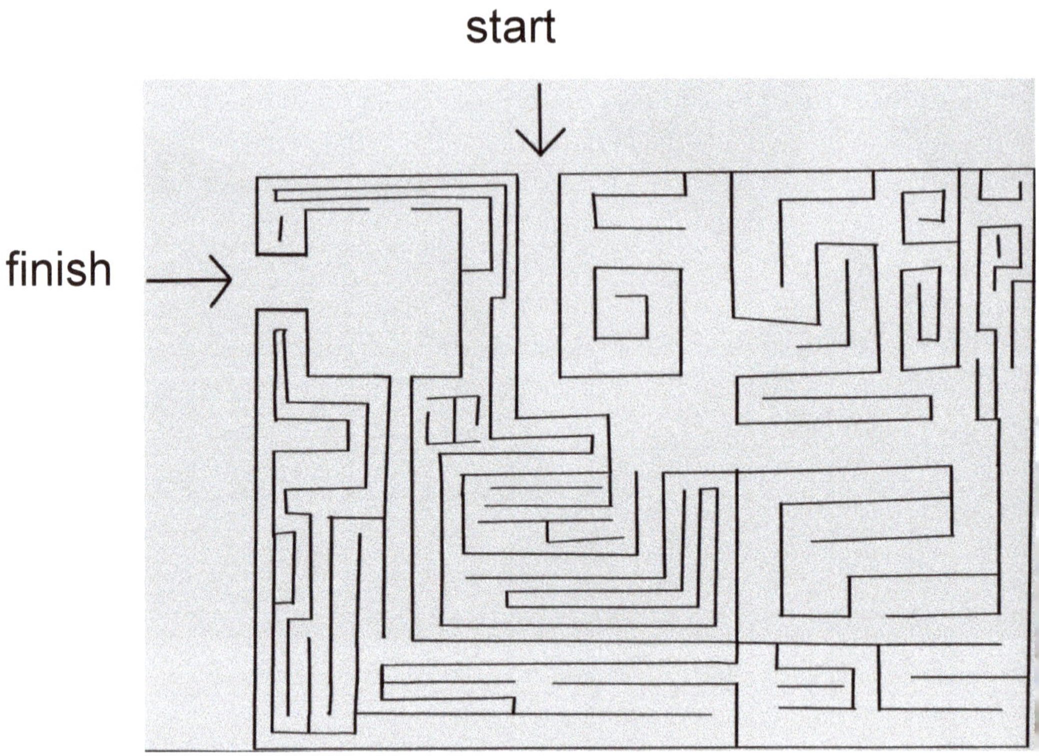

start

finish

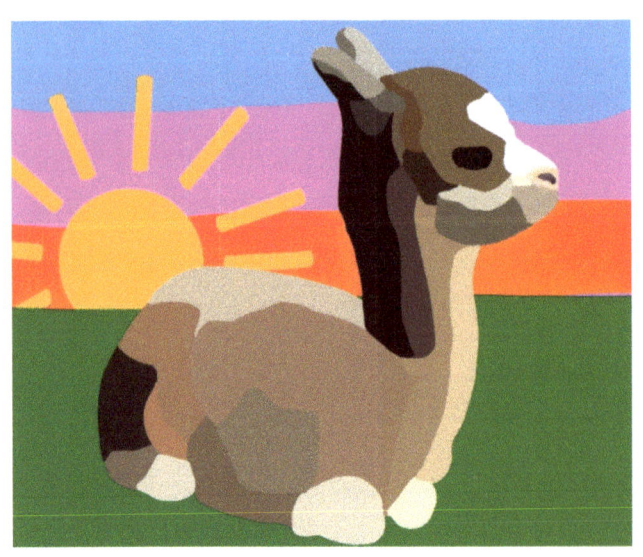

Llama Art by Leila

Cuttlefish are Important!!!
By: Annika, 10

Cuttlefish are cephalopods, in the phylum Mollusca. They are relatives of the octopus, squid, and nautilus. They are truly amazing creatures, and are my favorite animal!

Here are some interesting facts about cuttlefish:

1. *Cuttlefish are extremely intelligent.*
2. *They only live about nine months.*
3. *Cuttlefish can camouflage their entire body using cells called chromatophores. They can blend in with their background, and do impressive displays to mesmerize prey or attract a mate.*

They are also adorable. These pictures explain that!

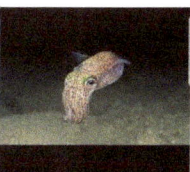

Cuttlefish have recently become an endangered species on the southern coast of Great Britain because of overfishing. Most of them are shipped overseas to countries where they are considered a delicacy. They could become endangered species in more places, if fishing continues without any limits.

Cuttlefish can seem a little odd when you first see one, but they are fascinating!

I love cuttlefish, and I hope you do too!!!

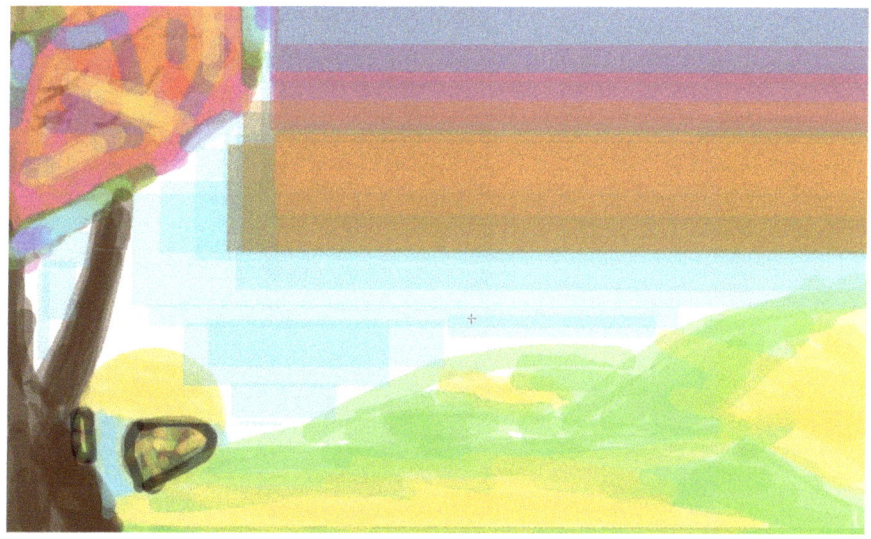

Art by Ava

Feathers and Fuzz- Artwork by Daniel peacock

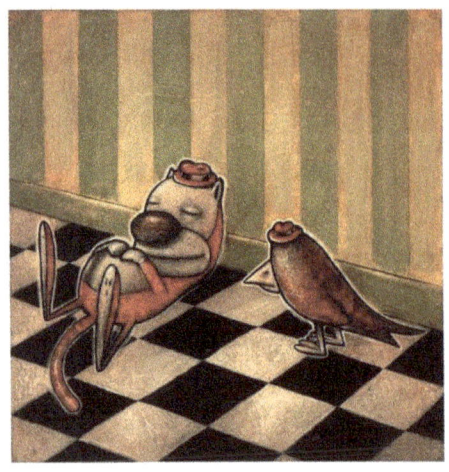

Detective Fuzz and and Detective Feathers

By Ava Muhlestein

It was a stormy night and Detective Fuzz and Detective Feathers were solving a case…" I'm serious it DID happen" said Furry the cat to the detective. Furry told the detectives that "someone stole the food in her fridge and keeps on stealing her stuff." Someone told Furry that Fuzz and Feather were good detectives. So she called and called all their emergency phones until finally they answered. Now all they had to do was go to Furry's house and stay over, all night keeping watch in case the thief came back. Fuzz insisted he go alone but Feathers knew he would fall asleep, so Feathers came along. Feather's was right, as soon as they went into Furry's house Fuzz fell asleep so Feathers woke him up. Five hours later Furry went to bed. And about three hours after Furry had fallen asleep, they heard something and then Feathers and Fuzz saw it! They saw Furry sleepwalking and eating all her own food. Case solved!

M&M Rainbow Art
by Luna Rose

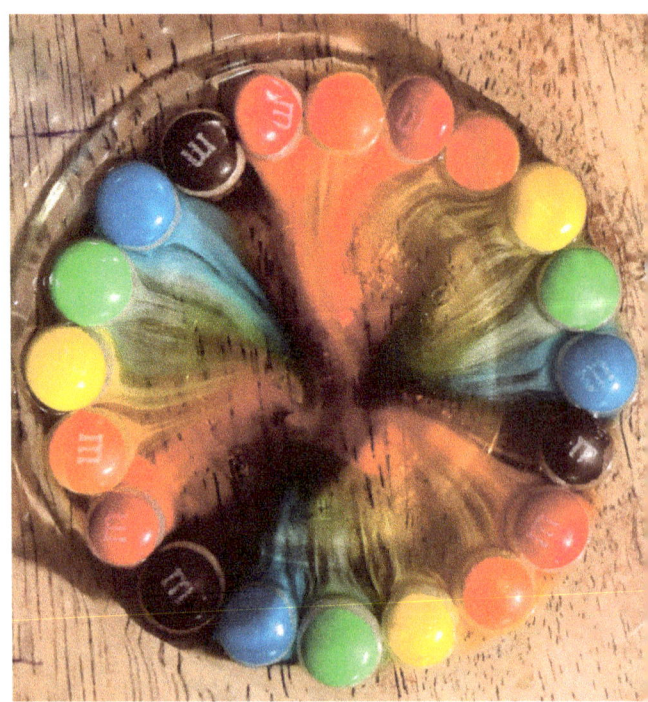

A Call to a Quest: Brothers
By Matthew Randolph

The sun shone down on Guidway city, bringing a warm feeling to all who inhabited it. The flowers of Ms. Wealer's tiny garden outside her window bathed in the sunlight and flourished as they had never. The tall, towering hill of the guideway guild which usually casted a gloomy shadow, now welcomed all who looked at it with open arms. When Eioffrey strode out of his door, he looked around himself and had a wonderful feeling and confidence that today was going to be a wonderful day.

Of course, he was wrong.

Eioffrey decided to start this day off by complementing Ms. Wealer on her exquisite flower bed and engaging her in a friendly conversation, and then heading off to where he always went at 8:00 am. Nightshade inn. Though the name was dark and brooding, today it sent off a jolly feeling. He opened the door with such confidence that Drugle, the village horror, gave him a toothy grin. Eioffrey sat down at his usual table with his friends Grog and Ivan. Grog was an Orc, and his hobby was cooking. Unlike the rest of his tribe, he viewed the pleasant side of everything. Ivan was a human like him, and, as Eioffrey thought, was a bit vain. He thought that Ivan was a bit presumptuous

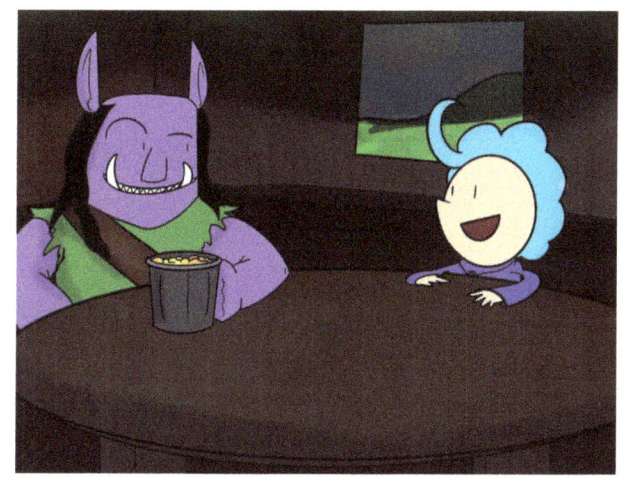

and headstrong, but admired him anyway. They had saved him a chair as usual, and already ordered him his juice. Though he was treated as an adult back at his home because he was rather big compared to the halflings, everyone here knew he was actually a kid, though he had the stomach of an adult.

"Lovely day, isn't it?" Grog inquired.

"Yes." Eioffrey replied. "Ms. Wealer's flowers look exquisite, don't you think?"

"You two sound like old ladies, talking about gardening." Ivan chuckled from his side of the table.

Old Flo rose from her seat across the room. "Hey, I take offense to that!" She shouted, picking up the first thing she saw and threw it at Ivan.

Fortunately, it was a newspaper, and it simply bounced off him. In a huff, Old Flo returned to her seat.

"I'm surprised that she heard that!" Eioffrey wondered quietly.

"I heard that too!" She yelled back.

Ivan sighed, picking the newspaper up from the ground and examining it. As Eioffrey sipped his juice, Ivan grew a shocked expression on his face. Eioffrey Looked up at him.

"What's wrong?" He asked.

Ivan laid the newspaper across the table. The headlining title was:

"NEW HEROES IN GUIDWAY"

And below it, the subtitle:

"QUARTZ SWORD STILL MISSING"

Grog leaned across the table. "That's us, right?" He said. Then, putting his fingers to his beard, said "But we didn't steal no sword...."

"Apparently not." Ivan replied. "It says here that a group of 'Heroes'" He raised his hands and did the quotation mark sign. "Saved a dwarf farmer named Jerome from a falling boulder, a few miles down."

"I know I don't know anybody named Jerome." Grog said.

"Anyway, after that, many people have been asking them for quests and stuff. They're calling themselves the 'Heroes of the Century'. That's all anyone knows about them."

He did the finger thing again and rolled his eyes.

"Speaking of quests, do we have any?" Eioffrey asked.

Ivan looked over to the Quest Board for the first time that day. It was completely vacant.

"I guess not." Grog sighed.

"I'm sure we can find some jobs if we look for them." Eioffrey said, patting Grog on the back.

Unfortunately, no one had any quests for them. The only 'quests' that anybody had were watering ms. Wealer's flowers while she ran errands, which Eioffrey obliged to, and washing Drugle's pantaloons.

After that chilling experience, the trio decided that they had enough of quests for that day. They decided instead, since these new heroes were rivals, to spy on them and find out how they did what they did. At first, they planned to hide where a disaster just might occur, such as Old Flo trying to reach her washing. But after two uneventful weeks, they pretty much gave up, until out came a newspaper with headlining title 'NEW HEROES TO MAKE APPEARANCE TODAY'. They packed all necessary needs and rushed off to the town square.

At first there was such a crowd that none of them could actually see the figures standing on the balcony, but as they got closer, they spotted them.

There was a half-reptile, half-human creature with eyes like a snake's, green skin, and an oily tail that flicked back and forth.

Behind him, there was an Ogre that had a scar over one eye that seemed permanently shut, and a thick wooden club. Atop his head was a tiny top hat that curled around the edges. It looked ridiculous.

But in front of them both was a short person with a violent beard and a coat of an owlbear. But Eioffrey recognized him without needing to see the coat, or the beard.

It was his brother.

Now, it wasn't his actual brother. It was his adoptive brother. When Eioffrey had been taken in by the halflings, Barvey was only two, and a rivalry quickly grew between them. Barvey knew all of his flaws and secrets and only kept them to himself for a reason Eioffrey never knew. But when Eioffrey spotted him, he seemed to turn to stone in place. Ivan spat on the ground, then turned to see Eioffrey as white as a ghost. After all, he hadn't seen Barvey after he disappeared one day. And seeing him now, it was like waking up to a different face. But soon, Barvey cleared his throat, and the crowd silenced.

"Good people of Guidway!" He said.

The crowd gazed intently at him.

"I would like to humbly thank you for taking time away from your daily schedule to meet us here! The Heroes of the Century!"

The crowd cheered, and Ivan spat on the ground again.

"Bosh." he muttered.

Someone in the crowd called "Thank you so much! We love you!"

Barvey grinned. "No, thank YOU! I'm so glad we could help! I can't even remember how much we've done for you!"

The reptilian creature pulled a piece of paper out of his pocket and unfolded it.

"Twenty-three questsssss, fifteen errandssss, piessss eaten: thirteen." He hissed.

Barvey laughed. "You've been keeping track?"

"You insssstructed me to."

Barvey glared at the reptile. He quickly folded the paper back into his pocket and kept quiet. Eioffrey wondered. How would three people who *obviously* worked poorly together succeed in so many quests? Not to mention, eating thirteen pies.

"Anyways," Barvey resumed. "I have something to tell you all! I know that with everyone giving us all the quests, everyone else must be bored out of their minds!"

"Yes we are." Grog mumbled.

"So I would like to hold a contest! Whoever wins gets to take the whole week's quests! Because they must be much better heroes than us!"

The Ogre spoke up for the first time.

"Huh!' He warbled. "Heroz!"

Barvey's smile cracked, but he somehow managed to regrow it.

Eioffrey suddenly felt a hand on his shoulder, and he turned around. It was Ivan.

"Come on." He muttered. "Let's get out of here."

The challenge was all anyone was talking about in town. Only a few people actually joined, as the Guild had few employees, many only beginners. Everyone else in Guidway just wanted to watch. They were like moths around a lantern. Always liked good betting. Eioffrey had no interest in that. After all, he was just a kid. Since the trio had left early, they had missed the rules. Thankfully, somebody had posted them over the Quest board. Though Eioffrey didn't care about the contest, Ivan was throwing an eternal fit.

"They can't just decide who gets quests!" He shouted. "That's the guildmaster's job! They're not even part of the guild!"

He picked up a random potion off the table of which they were studying them and threw it on the ground. The glass shattered and a cloud shaped like a Turkey leg emerged from the wreckage.

Eioffrey stared at the image before it disappeared. Then he turned to Ivan.

"Well, there's only one thing we can do to get our jobs back." He said. "Win the contest."

The next day, Ivan, Grog, and Eioffrey signed up for the contest, though Ivan gave the attendant the stink eye the whole time. As Eioffrey peeked at the list, he sighed. there were only four contestant teams, including them, and they all were all from the guild. After that, Ivan seemed to cheer up to the days leading up to the contest. On the day of the contest, all the competitors were summoned to the town square along with the rest of the village as well. There was a giant stage in the middle along with hundreds of chairs surrounding it. Once everyone had arrived, a goblin walked up onto the stage and reread the rules.

He cleared his throat. "Good people of Guidway." He coughed. He was old. "I am honored to present to you the most excitement we've had since that walrus juggled a few bananas a few months ago."

Eioffrey remembered the walrus. It was silly.

"But now we have excitement that is even greater!" He wheezed. "We have a challe-" His speech was interrupted by a sore throat. He flipped open a pocket and dropped a few pills into his mouth as the audience blankly stared at him.

He quickly resumed. "A Challenge!" He said, more vigorously.

The crowd cheered.

"The rules are simple." He continued. "We have two teams against each other battle in the ways of things that all teams must have!" He pulled out a list. "Swordsmanship, Magic, and Revivment!"

After the brief speech, the four teams stepped out of the crowd. Eioffrey had had no time the previous day to see exactly which teams had signed up. But now he got a pretty good look. One of the first teams was not a very experienced one. The name was team Fetchers and it consisted of a female elf, a dwarf, and a human. They would be easy to beat, for none of them had experience in Revivment. Next was a more intimidating team, team Bros. Three Orcs, all of them brutal and reckless. Their names were Jon, Jorah, and Francis. They were all brothers, and equally bloodthirsty. They would be hard to beat in combat. Finally there was one of the most elite teams in the guild team Chaneseek, consisting of a wizard named Aarvan, a Human named Orena, and a Goblin named Warby. Since they had experience in all fields, they would be hard to beat. The Old Goblin called attention again.

"Two groups of two teams will face each other. The groups that win will then fight each other. Then the group who wins that will challenge the Heroes of the century! If they win, they get first dibs on quests! If, not, the Heroes of the century will get first dibs as before."

"Heroes of the century." Ivan scoffed.

The four teams were split up. Thankfully, The trio was set with team Fetchers, the inexperienced team. There had been a bit of a delay at first, with the other team eeding to figure out which one of them would take part in Revivment. After that had been figured out, Ivan and the dwarf stepped up and unsheathed their swords. The goblin told them they had to knock the opponent off the ring to win. Once they started, the fight was fierce. Ivan would stab, then the dwarf. Finally, Ivan and the dwarf clashed swords, and pushed him back. As the dwarf landed outside the ring, a loud bell rang. The crowd cheered, and the dwarf stepped back up to scowl at Ivan. Next, Eioffrey and the elf participated in Magic. They stepped up, and the elf winked at him. He blushed, then realized elves were usually far older than they looked. This one was probably at least fifty, though she looked like she was something like fourteen. The goblin announced that the contestants needed to put on a performance and wow the crowd best they could. The elf stepped up, releasing a shower of fireworks. The crowd oohed. Eioffrey stepped up, shooting out a handful of Pink glowing flowers that exploded into a shower of millions of tiny petals that covered the audience. They cheered. The elf scowled, releasing at least twenty dragon-like shapes that twirled around, then joined together and exploded into an enormous dragon face. She turned to him.

"Let's see if you can do better." She whispered.

Eioffrey clamped his hands together, pulling out a seed. The elf stifled a snort. But just then, Eioffrey threw it in the air. It landed, causing a ripple effect. Suddenly, a tree sprouted from the place where the seed landed. The tree then grew hundreds of small bubbles that floated down the crowd. Some of them reached up and tried to pop them. As soon as the tree evaporated, the crowd cheered wildly. Eioffrey bowed, and the elf just crossed her arms and sulked off the stage. The contest was pretty much won from then. The human that was chosen to cook was pretty terrible at it. Apparently he had joined the team because of the elf. *Guess he doesn't know how old elves are.* Eioffrey thought.

While Grog made a delectable stew out of cabbage and dandelions, the human made a mess in his cauldron. Lizards legs, weeds, and random bits of meat floated around in his. The judges reluctantly handed Grog the badge without even needing to taste the human's.

When they began round two, team Chaneseek had beaten team Bros. Though team Chaneseek was more experienced, Eioffrey, Ivan, and Grog had more inventory. It was close, but the trio won. It had been boring at first, but now, knowing they were almost there, made them more confident.

Ivan was up first. He was to face the reptilian man, whose name was Iris. Iris was a swordsman.

Or is it Swordsnake? Eioffrey thought. It puzzled him.

When Iris and Ivan entered the ring, Iris' tongue flicked in and out. They drew their swords, and started fencing. Iris had a technique unlike any Eioffrey had seen. And by the looks of it, Ivan had never seen it either. Iris would strike, then jump back, preventing Ivan from getting a good shot at him. They continued this way for a while. Eioffrey noted that Iris stopped flicking his tongue. He wondered why, because snakes used their tongues for smelling. Eioffrey thought it would have helped Iris, but he seemed to be fine, dodging Ivan's blows.

The crowd started to get bored. A couple of people yawned and looked up at the sky. Suddenly, Eioffrey heard a noise. He turned to the ring, and saw Ivan blocking his eyes. Iris lunged at him, kicking him in the gut and sending him flying out of the ring. The crowd cheered as Eioffrey and Grog ran over to Ivan. As they helped him up, Ivan opened his mouth.

"He cheated." Ivan said.

Eioffrey was stunned. "How?"

Ivan got up shakily. "He flicked his tongue at the start. He was playing with me, moving me around. I was looking at him, and he flicked his tongue. There was some kind of light that blinded me. Next thing I know, I'm coughing up dust."

Eioffrey turned to Iris, who was slithering down the steps of the ring wearing a look of self-satisfaction.

"Ivan said you cheated." Eioffrey said.

"Ludicrousssss." Iris hissed. "How could I have cheated?"

Eioffrey stammered. He didn't know exactly how Iris could have cheated. Iris leaned down and flicked his tongue. A wide grin appeared on his face.

"Ssssssee?" He whispered.

Next was Revivment. Grog lined up with the Ogre, whose name was Oble. Oble's tiny hat was perched atop his head, threatening to fall at the slightest movement. Oble peeked at Grog with a discolored eye, making him flinch. Once it started, Oble and Grog started selecting certain items and dropping them into their cauldrons. But when Eioffrey looked closely, he saw that Oble would look at Grog's choice, then drop the same thing into his bowl, mixing it up a few times with other ingredients. Eioffrey tried to tell the judges, but he couldn't reach them.

When the Judges clambered up the steps, Eioffrey drew in a breath as they reached Oble's cauldron. They reached in a label and took a sip. The judge rose, made a face, and moved onto Grog's. Eioffrey Glanced at his brother who was glaring at Oble. The judges tasted Grog's, and smiled. Barvey-1, Eioffrey-1.

Eioffrey sat on his stool, thinking to himself. As far as he knew, Barvey had never practiced any magic. He didn't even have a pendant. He was wondering how he planned to win, but knowing Barvey, he probably had a nasty trick up his two-inch sleeve. As he stepped up onto the stage, he and his brother stood across from him.

Barvey smirked.

That was bad.

"Well." Barvey said, breaking the silence. "Hello, Eioffrey. Brother."

The crowd started whispering.

"Yes, tis true. Eioffrey is my brother. From Patapata town." He faced Eioffrey. "And he was the reason I left."

The crowd gasped. Clearly they disapproved of Eioffrey 'exiling' their 'savior'.

"Ever since, I've been wandering around. My only goal is to become a legend. And that meant becoming a hero."

He turned back to the crowd.

"It is also true that I have no experience in magic. But who needs magic, when this *fool* is using it so badly."

He jabbed a finger at Eioffrey. Eioffrey's brain started whirling, trying to figure out what he meant by that.

"I mean, look at him!" He continued. "Look at his hair!"

The crowd obliged.

"How do you think it got blue?"

Eioffrey covered his hair. He spotted Ivan and Grog looking at him curiously.

At the Halfling Village, Eioffrey had been conducting an experiment with the elder, Panch. During the experiment, an enormous explosion had left his hair swirly and blue.

And Now Barvey was retelling the whole story to the crowd, who were laughing all the while.

"My haaaaaair, my haaaaaaaiir!" Barvey yelled, doing an impression of Eioffrey. The crowd guffawed.

"Who do you want to be your hero?" Barvey asked the crowd.

"You! You! You!" The call rang out, getting louder. Eioffrey's pendant glowed with the rage that boiled inside of him.

"BARVEY! BARVEY! BARVEY!"

Eioffrey covered his ears to block out the horrid sound piercing his ears

"BARVEY! BARVEY! BAR-"

Suddenly, a giant rumble shook the ground and ceased the chanting. Everyone turned top where the source had come from, and found themselves looking at the mountain of Guidway Guild.

As the rumbling stopped, the stairs lining up to the top slid into the mountain, and a hole appeared in the bottom. A mist poured out from the hole as a figure exited.

The Guildmaster sure knew how to make an entrance.

Eioffrey had only met the Guildmaster once, and he had been drunk. Ivan, Grog, and him were applying for the Guild, and he gave them the position, without bothering to give a second glance.

But now, watching him in all his glory, staring back at the crowd, a shiver ran down his spine. The Guildmaster approached Barvey and threw back his hood.

"What is this!" Barvey yelled. "Get off my stage, old man!"

The crowd drew in a quick breath. Barvey looked around in confusion just as the Guildmaster swiftly kicked Barvey's leg from the back, pushed him into a leaning position, and threw Barvey's sword on the ground.

The Quartz sword. The one that had been missing for months.

The crowd gasped. Barvey's face went as cold as stone and desperately reached out to sheathe the sword, but the Guild master kicked it away. For an old man, he definitely was agile.

"Get off me, you fool!" Barvey yelled with a hint of terror in his tone. "Don't you know who I am?!"

The Guildmaster Glared at Barvey like an Eagle looking at a mouse it had been trying to catch.

"Don't you know who *I* am?" The Guildmaster hissed.

Barvey blinked.

"I run the guild. You have taken ownership of its rules when you were not allowed to. I was only alerted of it just now."

He turned to the crowd, casting a hateful shadow.

"And only Old Flo thought to tell me."

Old Flo stood up from the crowd.

"Hah! Payback!"

The Guildmaster turned back to Barvey.

"The Police will be very happy to get their hands on the thief of the Quartz sword."

The contest had crashed, and it was over. Barvey and his lackeys had been taken into custody. New rules had been appointed for the Guild, and from now on the Guildmaster would be a part of as much as he could. Old Flo received a reward, and now lived in a cottage at the top of a hill. Eioffrey's life had pretty much gone back to normal, but people would sometimes look at his hair.

A few days later, Eioffrey was in his cottage, which he shared with Grog and Ivan. Well, more like they shared it with him. it was pretty small. Flowers used to be on the window, but they died out quickly. They were replaced by a cactus. A portrait of a rather ugly woman that Ivan called 'Grammy' hung on the wall next to Grog's cooking equipment. Eioffrey had plenty of possessions when he left Patapata town to venture the world, but most of it was either stolen, used, or lost. His pendant was fortunate enough to escape that demise. Eioffrey's boots, soggy and muddy trudged on the welcome mat and he threw them in the pile of various unmatched shoes of different style and color. He sat down on the sofa they had found abandoned under rubble a few years ago. It let out a defiant moan as dust flew out from the bottom. He sat, looking at the clock's finger tick by before a knock at the door came.

Eioffrey sat up quickly. They almost never had visitors, and the Mailgoblin always left the stuff there. Eioffrey held his pendant steady and approached the door.

It was an officer.

Eioffrey blinked. This was the same kind of officer that held Barvey's arrest. The officer broke the silence.

"Someone wants to see you," He said, in a dry tone. "Before he leaves for jail for the next ten years."

Eioffrey knew who it was even before he stepped into the light.

Barvey.

"I want to apologize," Barvey said, hanging his head. "From then bottom of my heart."

Eioffrey stepped back.

"*What* heart?" Eioffrey asked. "Seems to me like you don't have one to apologize from. You lied to everyone. I didn't banish you. You disappeared."

Barvey took a deep breath.

"You did. Before you came, I was in the spotlight. Everyone adored me. Father was proud, mother said I was a prince. Then, you came. Discarded by the wretched humans you thought to be your parents. They were no parents. They left you all alone, a baby, in the Roaming woods to be fed upon. When father brought you in, everyone turned their focus on you. I was no longer a star, a prince that father and mother cherished. They were always like: 'Be nice to your brother' and 'you're too old for that'. So one day, I left. I felt as if I had no more meaning there. I stumbled upon those two idiots," He said, jabbing his finger at Oble and Iris. "Ever since, I've been trying to become a star again. Seems I've taken the wrong path, though.

He sighed, looking down at his feet. Eioffrey looked at him. They stayed like that for a long time.

"Finish up!" One of the guards said, tapping on the window.

Eioffrey turned to the window, then back to Barvey.

He walked forward, and hugged him.

Barvey stiffened up, but paused, and embraced him.

They stood there for a minute. The guards eventually came back in, and took Barvey back.

"Eioffrey?" Barvey said.

Eioffrey turned his head.

"I love you."

Eioffrey smiled.

"I love you too."

[Facts About Rabbits](#)
By Leila

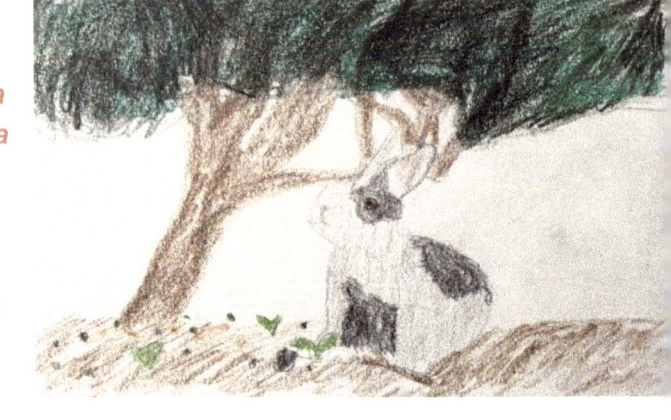

1) A female rabbit is called a doe, a male rabbit is called a buck, and a baby rabbit is called a kit.

2) More than half the world's rabbits live in North America.

3) A rabbit's teeth never stop growing.

4) Rabbits perform an athletic leap known as a binky when they're happy, performing twists and kicks in mid air.

ANIMAL WORD SEARCH by Leila Goldstein

CAT, DOG, LEMUR, BEAR, CHEETAH, WOLF, FOX, RABBIT, HUMAN, COW, SHEEP, PIG, LLAMA, TIGER, KANGAROO, LION,

C	L	E	M	U	R	D	H	K	L	H	A	R
O	A	B	R	P	M	A	R	I	P	I	K	D
W	L	T	L	B	B	E	A	R	R	M	O	P
H	I	P	H	I	L	K	B	H	K	R	K	N
B	L	L	A	M	A	I	B	U	H	P	H	A
M	P	K	P	M	A	D	I	M	P	F	W	L
L	R	M	C	H	E	E	T	A	H	D	O	G
A	R	K	I	H	L	I	A	N	L	A	L	X
R	I	P	I	G	A	R	I	A	R	A	F	B
P	I	K	A	N	G	A	R	O	O	M	L	A
B	M	B	H	B	I	K	S	H	E	E	P	I
D	R	L	I	P	H	I	K	M	D	P	R	A
L	P	M	T	I	G	E	R	I	B	A	A	P

Fun Facts on Elephants

Facts & Art By: Ava Muhlestein 10yrs old

Q: Why do Elephants have wrinkles? A: The wrinkles are to store water, so they stay hydrated.

Q: Why do Elephants not get hurt when they step on twigs? A: They have pads on their feet

Silly but true:
Did you know Elephants are actually afraid of mice!

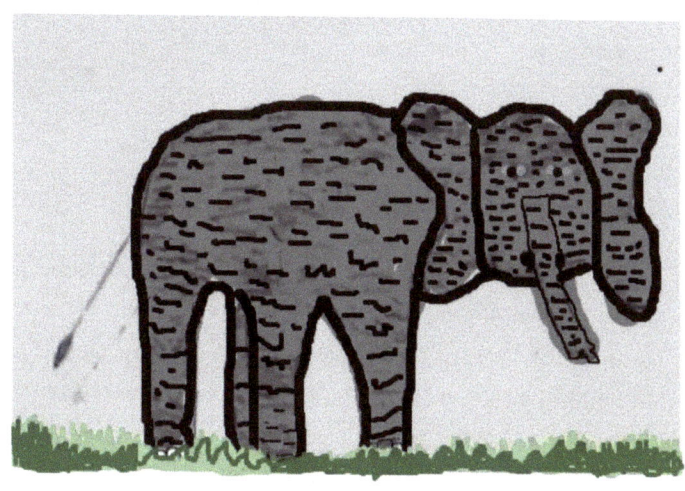

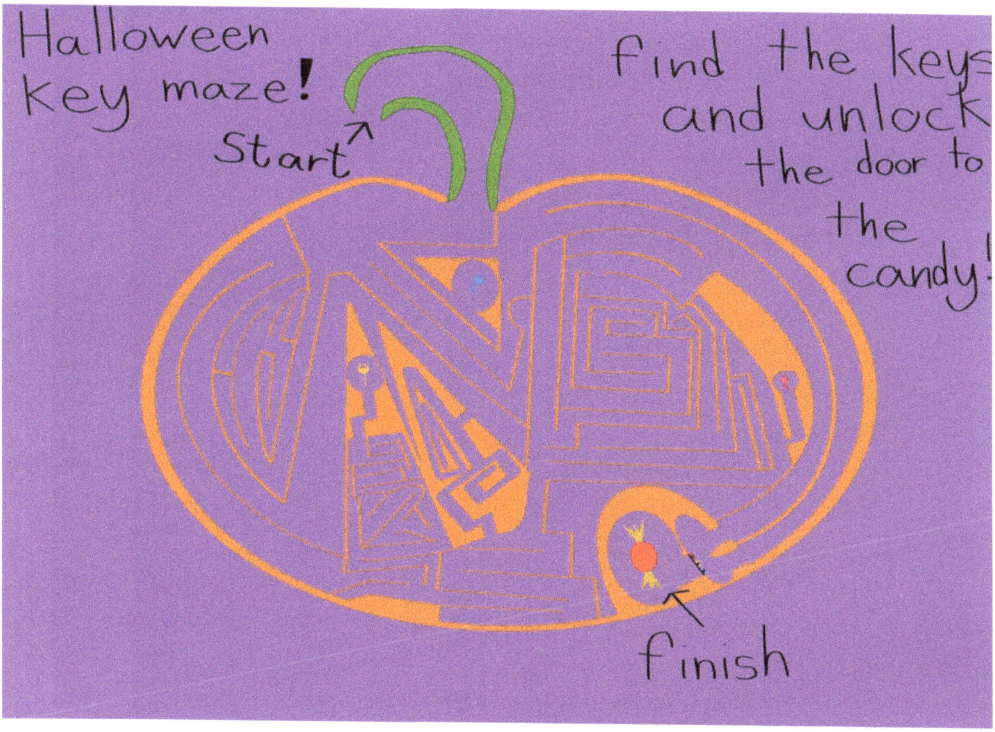

Art By: Leila

The Journal of the Dragon: A Story
By James Clawson

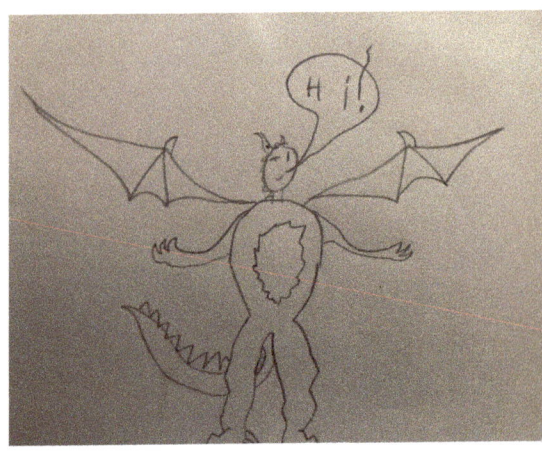

Hi. I'm the prince. Yeah, right. I'm the dragon. Obviously, because I joked I'm the prince. But, I'm the dragon...trust me. I'm not lying. Anyways, anybody that didn't create this amazing magazine is probably pretty...confused. So, I'll just act like this is brand new. Just imagine this: fantasy story, merged with an adventure modern times story. Make sense? No? Okay, um...okay. Just read and I'll make sure that it kinda...makes sense. Anyway, at around 11:00, everyone was sitting around a campfire.

"So…" said James, awkwardly. That was because there was that part of the movie where everyone was tired and nobody was talking. Prince was getting tired of this, so in a sarcastically excited voice, he said:
"So, who is everyone's favorite, um...person?"
"You mean like, among us?" said james.
"Yeah! I'll go first." said the prince. "My favorite person is...Dragon!"
the dragon immediately started blushing and hid himself in his wings. But he still decided he'd go next. "My favorite person is...Goblin.'
"Okay, he's not even here but I guess he still counts." said James. "Your turn, Princess."
The princess said: "Easy! Mysel-"
"Nope." said James.
"Aw...fine. Um...I guess prince."
"REALLY?" said the prince.
"No." said the princess. Then it was James's turn.
"Well, mine is-"
That's when the earthquake happened. A monstrous blob slowly moved towards the camp site. Then, the handmaid came running. "(huff...huff) the…(huff...huff) the blob is coming…(huff...huff..)" she said.
The handmaid is the princess's...hand maid. She loves to read books, and kinda just agrees with everything the princess says. Also, rumor has it she knows the princess's book secret...
Anyway, the crew was shocked to hear that a blob was coming. James got together all his magic spells that he learned from the wizard, the princess got her sword ready, the dragon

was ready to shoot some fire, and the prince went to Taco Bell to get some burritos. His excuse was "We need fuel to fight!"
I don't know where he gets this stuff.

Anyway, there came the blob. Suddenly, it grew monstrous arms and slapped the dragon.
The dragon looked back at the blob and his eyes became furious. He shot a fireball but missed.

James shouted a spell: "Freeze!" as the princess chopped its arm off. As soon as James used the spell, the blob stopped moving. The dragon had a clear shot.

He blew the blob's head right off and the blob dissolved into nothing.

Just then, James heard a crunch. It was the prince snacking on some chips.

"Hi, guys!" he said.

"Were you just watching us fight off that giant blob?" the princess said.

"Yeah. watching people fight a blob doesn't really leave a lot of options for helping." Prince said.

The Four Seasons Poem
By: Leila & Annika.

Summer
It's not a bummer when it's summer
The flowers are bright, the clouds are white
The sky is blue, bluebirds are too

Fall
I like fall but it's not best of all
The leaves are red but some are dead
You might need to rake or fish in the lake

Winter
Winter is winter the snow grows bigger
It's cold and very old
Each season it's new under the ice is blue

Spring
Spring makes me sing
Spring means dancing
Trees and bees
Growing grass and mowing grass

BOOK RECOMMENDATIONS & WHY!

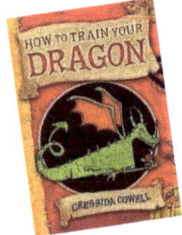

Crispin: Septimus Heap series, How to Train Your Dragon series, A Series of Unfortunate Events

Ava: Till Tomorrow Mr. Marsworth, Sparrow Road, Diary of a Wimpy Kid, Dog Man, Dork Diaries, Geronimo Stilton.

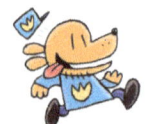

Leila: keeper of the lost cities, by: Shanon Messenger. Keeper of the lost cities is a good book because each character is different. It's a book about a girl who finds out that she is a elf. &
Percy Jackson, by: Rick Riordon. Percy Jackson is about a kid whose father is the greek god poseidon.

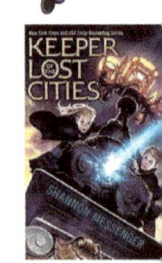

Luna: The Land of Stories, By: Chris Colfer, The Land of Stories is a book about two twins who find out about a whole new world at their fingertips . The Land of Stories was the first actual book I ever read and it's very special to me.

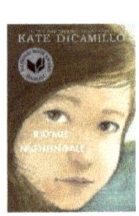

Tracy: Raymie Nightingale by Kate DiCamillo
In Raymie Nightingale, I love how author Kate DiCamillo artfully creates a friendship between three girls through a series of unusual events. The humor in these stories is my favorite part, but it is also a bittersweet story.

Annika: Mandy
An amazing book by Julie Andrews Edwards!
It's about an orphan named Mandy. She is sweet, kind, and a bit mischievous! She finds her own little place not far from the orphanage, and she finds pros and cons along the way to making it her own!
I love that it Introduces many sweet, kind, funny, and curious characters along the way! I also love that Mandy is experiencing many different changes as the story unfolds! There is always something that makes you want to turn the page!

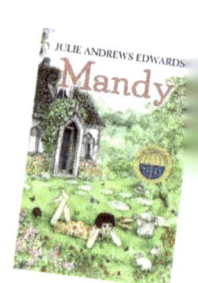

The Goblin Forest
by Crispin, 11.

INTRODUCTION

Hi there. I'm Ava, and I have never gone cliff diving in my WHOLE ENTIRE LIFE. So unfair. I have long brown hair, am twelve years old, and have been scared of snakes for as long as I can remember. I'm okay with worms though. I love being outside and getting dirty, which is why I wear jeans and a ragged T-shirt at all times. Once, at my aunt's wedding I wore a dress, and that wedding officially counts as the Worst Day Of My Life, but still. Not the point. Okay. Let's get on with the story.

CHAPTER 1, I GO INTO THE FOREST

One day, I was walking down Main Street on my way home from school, when I saw Kelsey heading straight towards me. Now ordinarily, I would be brave and walk right past her, but today was NOT a good day to do that. For one thing, I owed her 20 dollars. 20 dollars that I didn't have. 20 dollars that I was supposed to pay her two days ago. I looked behind me. No escape. And THIS is why I decided to take a shortcut. I ducked down the one alley I knew she wouldn't dare follow me down. Technically I wasn't supposed to go down it either, but this was a dire situation. Now, there was actually nothing forbidden about the ALLEY, although it was rather dark and dripping. The reason it was off-limits was because it led to the FOREST. I have never been a big fan of forests, but particularly the Goblin's Forest. No one actually knows where the Goblin part came from, but there's always been something off about it. I was hoping that if I wandered around in the forest long enough, I would find a way out. Now, looking back on this, that probably wasn't the wisest choice, but for some reason, a creepy dark forest sounded infinitely better than a middle school girl. Anyway, I could always use my phone to call for help. Uh oh. My phone. I had left it in my locker at school. I ran through the contents of my backpack in my head: Empty paper lunch sack, gym socks, jump rope. I always bring my own jump rope. A lighter from science class! Light! I wasn't really supposed to *take* the lighter, but it sure would come in handy now. looked up suddenly, and I was at the end of the alley. I took a breath, and plunged into the forest.

I looked around. Pretty dark. Kinda spooky. Suddenly, a bird began to sing. Well, "sing" is the wrong word for it. More like, "screech dementedly". As I looked around, in the dim light I could make out a huge shape perched on a branch. It had shiny, glittery, metallic scales, but this was what really freaked me out: *It appeared to have a human face!* It looked at me with cold, lamplike yellow eyes that seemed to peer into the depths of my soul. It gave one last scream, then disappeared into the shadows.

TO BE CONTINUED...

The "Mona Lisa"

By Annika, 10

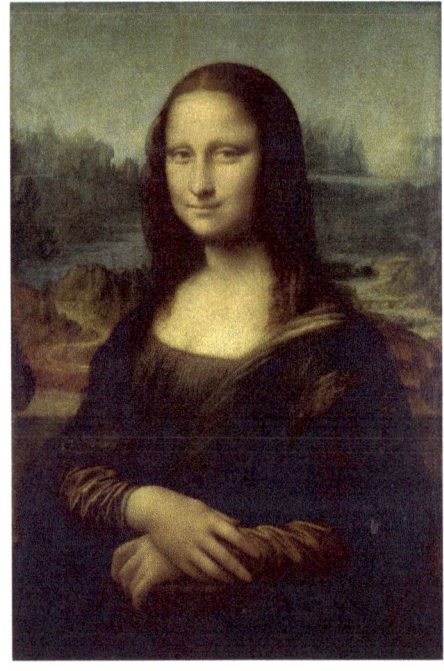

Mona Lisa seems to be the woman in this painting. In the background, we can see a river, some trees, and a clear, fading sky. Mona Lisa might be standing in front of this background, getting a painted portrait of herself. This is an Incredible art piece!

"Mr. da Vinci?" Asked Mona Lisa. "You must paint my picture!" She said. "A-Alright." Mr. da Vinci replied. So he painted Mona Lisa's portrait. It took a lot of work and paint, but the job was done. It was BEAUTIFUL! It became famous world-wide! "You have been good to me." Said Mona Lisa. "I will be eternally grateful." A small smile came upon her face. And that smile, ment a lot to Mr. da Vinci. "I will paint for you anytime you need me! I love to paint!" Mr. da Vinci replied. "Thank you." Mona Lisa said with a grin. Mona Lisa and Mr. da Vinci were good friends for many years. They posed and painted all day, every day! That is the true story of Mona Lisa.

Fruity Word Search
by Leila Goldstein

Apple, pear, mango, plum, peach, banana, lime,

A	P	P	L	E	J	I
F	D	L	E	I	P	O
S	Q	S	U	A	M	R
G	E	D	L	M	C	E
T	O	M	A	T	O	H
A	B	A	N	A	N	A
M	A	N	G	O	X	H

Above Writing Inspired by The Mona Lisa by Leonardo di Vinci

Once upon a hidden place
By: Luna Rose

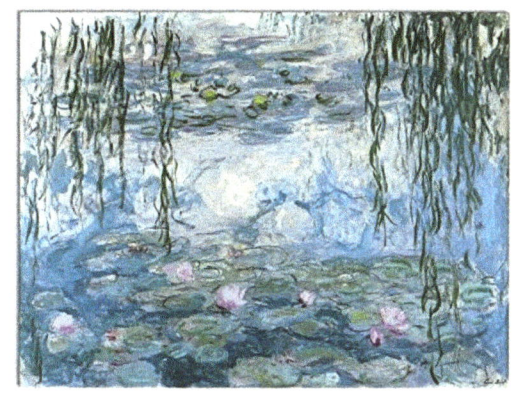

Once there was a group of fairies, there were the river fairies, lava fairies, cloud fairies, and stone fairies.

There was a group of four friends, one from each clan. The stone fairy's name was Dirtana. The river fairy's name was Lily pandit. The lava fairy's name was Magma, and the cloud fairy's name was Airleth, but her friends called her airhead.

"HEY MAGMA! BET YOU CAN'T GET TO THE END OF THE STREAM BEFORE ME!" Lily pandit said. She had gills instead of wings. She wore a silky turquoise dress with a lavender headband and her blackish blue hair went down to her waist.

"No fair, you know lava fairies harden when they touch water!" Magma complained. She was wearing a dark red jumpsuit, and her strawberry red hair was in a ponytail, instead of wings she had a torch stuck to her back and it only burned out when she wanted it to.

"THAT'S YOUR PROBLEM! NOT MINE!" Lily pandit said, already spreading her gills.

"Well I think one of you should make a mud pie so we can have a pie chucking contest!" Dirtana said as she smiled. She had on a brown ripped t-shirt with jeans, and her dark brown hair was in braids.

"SOME OF US LIKE TO BE CLEAN!" Airleth shouted as her wings flapped her higher. She had on a white tunic and her blond hair was in a waterfall braid.

Writing Inspired by Monet's "Water Lilies"

The Summer Fairy
By Leila Goldstein

Once upon a time there was a fairy who lived in a flower. One day, she was sitting in her flower thinking about how much she loved summer and how little summer was left. She peeked out of her flower; it looked like a perfect day, but it was the last day of summer. Where she lived the season changed very fast, so it wasn't a good idea to go outside--if it changed while she was outside she could get covered in leaves! She stopped looking outside and began to think about what she would even do when fall came. Her thoughts were interrupted by a loud rustle, it sounded like leaves falling. She was too scared to look out of her flower, so she just listened as the beautiful green leaves of summer turned red and orange and fell to the ground. When the sound stopped, she bravely looked out of her flower and saw reds and oranges. Summer never had so much of those colors--it was very pretty, and it wasn't so bad. Then she went outside to go play hide and seek with the other fairies.

The end

Poetry By Leila & Annika

Purple
Purple purple the color will swivel
The color likes to play all day, if you don't hold it tight it will float away.
The color of some lilies, it's a good color if you are silly.
Oh the beauty of purple flowers, purple has a lot of powers.

Black
Black cat black hat,
black is not a bad choice, it has a strong voice.
It will cover all the other colors,
You need a lot of color to cover black paint.

"Normal"
An excerpt from a new novel by Luna Rose

<u>Prologue</u>

It was rainy outside Anzly's bedroom window. Anzly could hear her dad's old timey record player down stairs, it was playing Jingle bells which to Anzly made no sense because it was Fall.

Anzly opened her window and stuck her hand outside in the rain, the rain dripped onto her hand and she thought how each and every raindrop was splashing her hand, and how it made a pattern, *Pit pat, pit pat, pit pat.*

Anzly closed the window and got up from the hopechest she was sitting on. She walked over the pile of homework she had dumped on her floor and then she got to her bookcase, she took out an old jewelry box, the jewelry box was light brown and if jewelry boxes could have age spots then this one did. The jewelry box used to be Anzly's grandma's but then her grandma died so the jewelry box had gone to Anzly. Anzly had kept pictures of her friends and her in it and a picture of some of her family but she just mainly liked looking at it. She picked up a picture of herself when she was thirteen and noticed her hair hadn't changed.

In the picture Anzly's hair went down to her shoulders and was a shade of brown that looked like it was from a tree, but it wasn't, Anzly was wearing a sky blue jumpsuit that had no sleeves and had dark blue flowers on it.

"ANZLY IT'S TIME FOR DINNER!" Anzly's mother called from down stairs. As Anzly got to the kitchen she saw her mom. Anzly's mom had blond hair that was almost always in a loose ponytail, and she wore a baby blue button down shirt with black leggings.

"What are we having?" Anzly asked.

"SPAGHETTI!" Anzly's little brother Max yelled as he jumped out from behind the couch. Max was wearing a red t-shirt and his blond hair was short and curly.

"AND LEMONADE!" Anzly's other brother Jay said as he jumped out from under the table. Jay was wearing a black t-shirt with camoflash shorts, and his blond hair went down to his shoulders.

"WE ARE HUNGRY!" Both of Anzly's brothers said as they put their arms up.

"Anzly can you set the table please?" Anzly's mother said after she stopped laughing at the boys still posing with grins on their faces.

"Okay."

After Anzly set the table she walked over to her dad. Anzly's dad was a tall man who always wore a white fancy shirt with black work pants and a tie, and his blond hair was always in a buzz cut.

Anzly had always wondered why she was the only one in her family with brown hair. Once she asked her mom but her mom had just changed the subject.

"How is my almost fifteen year old?!" Anzly's dad said as she sat on his lap.

"Good." Anzly replied.

"You want to look at the stars. ?" Her dad said.

"Sure." Anzly said as she got up. Her and her dad sat on the porch and looked up at the sky. Anzly saw a shooting star and let her eyes follow it to the other end of the street. There stood the Beller's house. It had broken windows and the house gave Anzly nightmares. She hated the house, but there it stood tall, crooked and creepy.

HORRORSCOPE
By Crispin Campbell

January- Today is NOT a good day to summon demons. If you do, it will end with disaster.

February- Every spell you do today will do the EXACT OPPOSITE of what you're trying to do.

March- If you encounter a dragon today, IT WILL EAT YOU.

May- If you get abducted by aliens today, do not worry! Their ship will crash on Mars, where you will join a friendly Martian colony.

June- If you see a glowing door in the forest, don't go in.

July- If you fly your broomstick today, try not to hit any trees. If you do, you will break your leg.

August- If you fall into a portal to another dimension, IT WILL NOT BE A NICE DIMENSION.

September- Do not try to steal an ogre's treasure, or you will be turned into soup, eaten raw, or baked into Human Nuggets.

October- Do not try to raise the dead. We are not kidding.

November- Do not stow away on a ghost ship, because, well, ghost ship.

December- DO NOT forget goblin repellent.

Limbo- If you are unlucky enough to be stuck in a time warp, we have no advice to offer.

Published by Sorcerer Press

Frail But Fearless
By: Annika Arvik & Luna Randolph
~~~~~~~~~~~~1~~~~~~~~~~~~

Down deep, deep in the darkest of places. Not a good spot for a human, but a great spot for a Frail.
Frails are like fairies, but they don't have wings or magic. They are just little people who don't use metal, plastic or any of that stuff, they just use nature. It was raining hard! Just amazing!
"This is the most fun I've had since last rain season!" Misteria yelled. She was in a slick, blue, purple and green leaf gown, her hair was dark Blueish black, and she loved rain! "You should join us!"

"No thanks, I'm an Air Frail! Unless you forgot!" Fly said. He was in a purple shirt, with plain green pants. He had dirty blond hair, and he was bored at the moment.
"Oh, come on, Fly!?" Falls shouted. She had long, dark black hair, with a gown that was rather green. She had a sash going around it in a most lovely way!
"We are civilized children, Civilized!" Fly chanted, still feeling had a shred of dignity.
"NOPE!!!" Misteria yelled. She grabbed Fly's arm and drenched him in the muddy dew on the ground. Fly came up gasping for air, feeling offended.

"How dare you! WE ARE CIVILIZED!!!"
"We are so not!" Falls shouted.
"So just have fun!"
"Fine" Fly said (calmer) "But ONLY because there is no hope of salvaging this leaf shirt.'"

So in the end of that, Fly learned to loosen up a bit. But the night eventually got better. Everyone seemed to be arriving at the (castle). It was the tallest tree that represented all of the tribes. On the tree, scattered everywhere, were the Nature Frail's greatest creations, mushrooms. They were yellow and looked like circles cut in half. And for the Water Frail's part, there was a lovely stream that went all around the wondrous tree. For the Air Frail's symbol, they put lily pads in the water, and clouds in the sky around the branches of the tree. And the announcement began. Everyone huddled around one big mushroom, where the leader of the Frails was speaking. She was wearing a lovely dress with all different kinds of crystal embroidered on it. She was the only crystal Frail in existence!
"Everyone, I am pleased to tell you that we just discovered….Two new tribes of Frails!" Everyone cheered with excitement.

"And here they are!" The first kind of new Frails had brown hair and dresses made out of stones, they had black or brown hair and they had splashes of moss everywhere.

"These are the Rock Frails! And what they are going to add to this giant tree, is a stone bridge, so none of us have to swim across the moat." Everyone cheered en louder than before. The next tribe suddenly appeared, they had fire for hair and had dresses that were made of roses and the dresses were signed at the bottom. and looked to be quite useful. "These are the Fire Frails!" No one was expecting Fire Frails any time soon, so it felt like there was a whole new world out there, suddenly when the announcement was over,

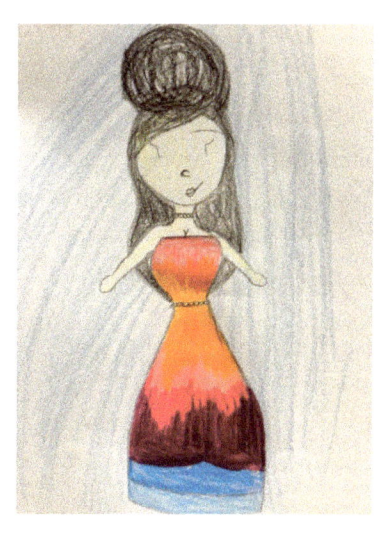

everyone rushed to the Fire Frails and not one Frail payed any attention to the other new-comers. But one Frail did…Brazil.

Brazil was Fly's older sister, always wanting to get rid of him. She was an Air Frail. She wore a long dress that went down to her feet, at the top were lots of layers of purple fading into another just before it reached the bottom. At the bottom were prints of lily pads. And she had light, blond, hair. She walked over to a girl who looked to be her age and said hello.

"Hi" "Hi" the girl replied shyly. "I'm Brazil."
"I'm Bouldeweth." She said. "I don't know if I will ever like this place without a soft warm welcome." Bouldeweth mumbled.
"I know, it stings but-wait a minute, your right! I never really did get a good welcoming when my tribe was new! Well, it seems you're right, this place isn't fit for us, we should go somewhere new!" "Do you mean, like "run away"?" Bouldeweth asked. She was so amused and felt like running away was the plan for her. "What! No, I mean just go on a vacation with other Frails, they will see how amazing *you* are, and forget all about those Fire Fonease."

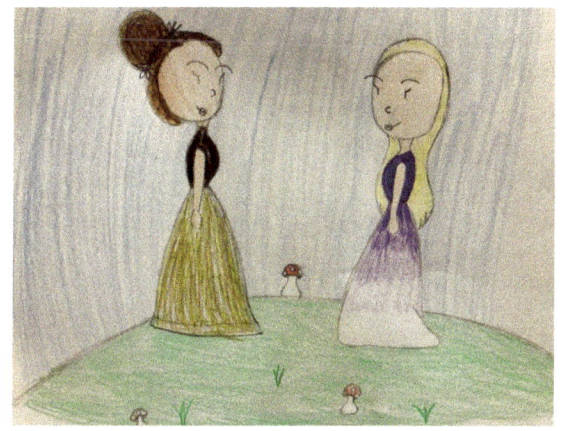

"Well….n-ok. Fine, I guess I could try." Bouldeweth said, dropping all amusement. "Well, let's go in the morning, come on! Your cabin is next to mine!" Brazil said in excitement. She was so happy to have gained an actual friend.

The Halloween Thief (an excerpt)
By Leila Goldstein

"Trick or treat!" I said it very happily, I always looked forward to Halloween for the whole year. Mr. Mutton's yard was decorated with pumpkins and scarecrows and he usually gave the best candy. But this time Mr. Mutton didn't give me candy. Instead he said, "trick."

"What?" I said. I had never heard anybody say that.

Suddenly, all the scarecrows seemed more alive, and I realized that they were moving toward me. Then a UFO was above me--don't ask me how it got there or what was going on because I didn't know. I ran all the way to my house. Whatever that was I did *not* want to be part of it.

That night when I was in my bed I heard a loud VROOM! *"It sounds like a UFO that steals cows,"* I thought. But I was not a cow so I didn't worry very much, and I went back to sleep.

But when I woke up, I was not in my bed. *"Maybe I AM a cow,"* I thought, *"in that case I am in BIG trouble."*

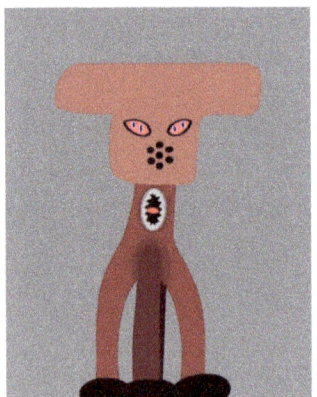

In front of me was someone or something that was not a human. It had a T-shaped head, its mouth was on its chest and it had two normal legs but it also had two extra legs, one on the front of its body and one on the back.

"Are you going to eat me?!?" I said.

"No, no!" it said. "I am a berg; bergs are vegetarians. My name is Nark, and you are a human, are you not?"

"Yes, I am a human, but why did you take me out of my bed in the middle of the night?" I asked.

"We need the help of a human child, and you were the best child we could find. That neighbor of yours, Mr. Mutton, is working for Lee Garbonzo."

Lee Garbonzo was the owner of the Mississippi Company; he was so rich he had bought the Mississippi River.

Nark continued, "And, we need to have someone small enough to fit through the vent in Lee Garbonzo's Research Facility for Stealing Halloween."

"Stealing Halloween!?!" I asked. I was so confused.

Maybe Nark is the one who is actually trying to steal Halloween! But why would he want Halloween? I decided to trust him, because why would he lie?

"I will help you." I said. "But how will he steal Halloween?"

"Lee Garbonzo is very rich, so he can use his money to buy Halloween from the government. I know this because I can shape shift, and I shifted into one of the workers working for Lee Garbonzo." said Nark.

"But Halloween is not owned by the government, and if you need someone small, why can't you just shape shift into someone my size?" I asked.

"I can't shift into anything smaller than myself."

That was very strange because he looked like he was about seven feet tall, though I was only four feet and nine inches, so maybe I thought he was taller than he was.

Fairies

By: Ava Muhlestein Age, 11

Chapter 1 part 1

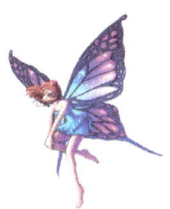

"Once upon a time in a place far, far away from here lived a unicorn named ... actually I don't know what her name was, I think it's Cora,sorry Amy." Lily Looked at her watch ,
"Mom and Dad will be home soon. Amy, it's almost your bedtime." Lily said patiently. "Ok, but can you read to me tomorrow?" Said Amy. " That's fine but you have to listen." Said Amy." "Ok" said Amy, and she went to bed. Lily was just about to turn on her favorite show, The Kitten who plays Football, when she heard Amy shout ..."Lily! Come quick! There is a fairy in my room!"

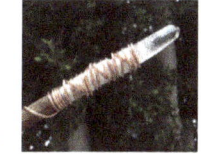

"Amy, there is no such thing as fairies. It's probably just a fly" said Lily, and waited for Amy to respond, but instead she heard "CREEK", so she ran upstairs and saw Amy's bedroom window open... and Amy wasn't in it! "AMY! ARE YOU HERE?!!" said Lily, holding the fairy wand that Amy had gotten her for her birthday last year. Lily was only 10 years old, she had nothing else to use to protect herself if someone were to jump out and grab her. Then, she saw a bright light coming from the closet...

Chapter 2 part 2

"Was Amy right?" She thought "Were there really Fairies?". Lily was watching the light. Just then, the light turned pink! And then... red? She knew something was not right, so she opened the closet door to find a circle swarming with colors around it . It looked as if it had a picture of a small village inside, only fairy sized. She knew at that second, Amy would have gone in there if she saw it. The picture seemed to be shrinking. If she ever wanted to see her sister again, she had to jump.

Chapter 3 part 3

"It's not fair." Amy thought. "I'm 6 And Lily is 10, we're almost the same age, yet I am not allowed to stay up, maybe my wand would help. My mom said it's got magic in it, like in me.

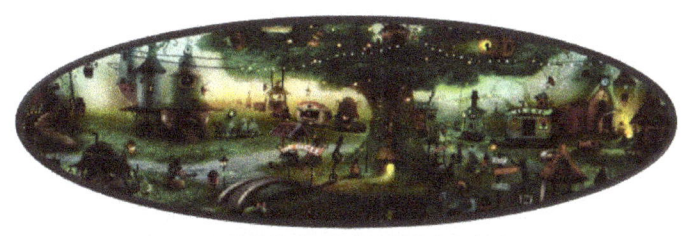

"Magic wand, make a fairy." said Amy. All of a sudden, the window opened and in flew a fairy. "LILY!! THERE IS A FAIRY IN MY ROOM!!" Amy ran into the bathroom and waited, then she came out to see a portal... just then it closed.

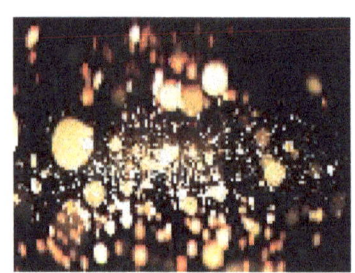

Amy went into her room to find her wand on the floor, not on her bed .... "Oh no, LILY is in the portal!" Amy grabbed her wand and made a wish to open the portal. To be continued...

Sunrise
By Crispin
The sun shines bright on
The beautiful golden hill
All is peaceful

Desperately Trying To Write A Limerick
By Crispin
There once was a dog named Matt,
That liked to scare the cat,
He liked to chew,
On an old blue shoe,
and that (I think) is that.

Haiku
By Crispin
Fish- flavored ice cream
Is there anything grosser?
Hummus popsicle

My First Haiku (and the beginning of my haiku debut)
By Crispin
I can't write haiku
It is too hard for me
I will not write one

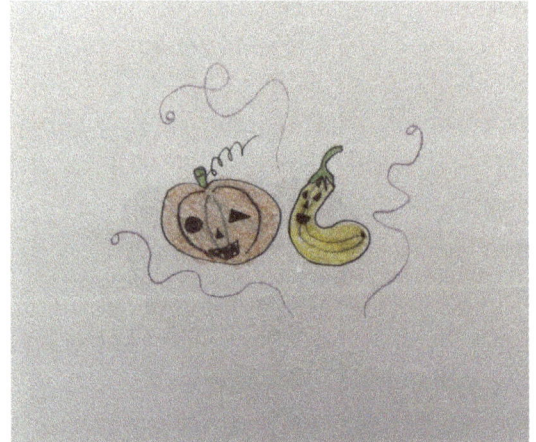

Fall *Art by Annika*

Relatively Ridiculous Haiku That I Am Writing Because I Can't Think Of Anything Else To Write About
By Crispin
Once upon a time
There was a haiku
It was this haiku

Bon Appetit Treat!
By Annika

Ingredients:
1. *(Any berries you have)*
2. *Chocolate*

Things you'll need:
1. *A bowl*
2. *A spoon*

Bon Appetit Treat Steps:
1: Bring the bowl.
2: Put all of the berries you want into the bowl.
3: Mix the berries, using the spoon.
4: Break up the chocolate.
5: Put the chocolate in the bowl and mix.

ENJOY YOUR SNACK!

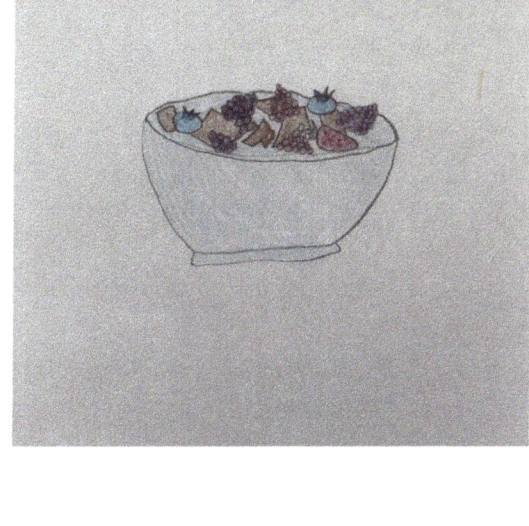

Starry night

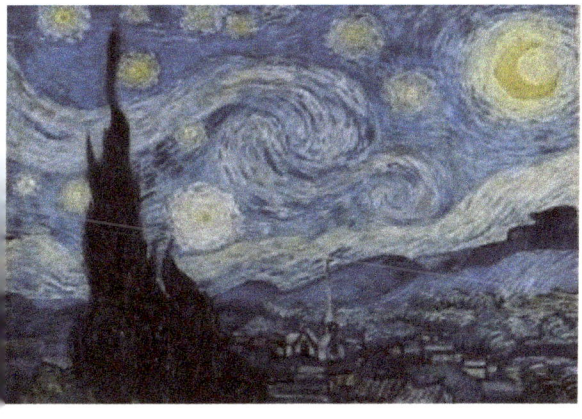

By Leila Goldstein

Everyone is asleep,
No one can see,
Look at the houses quieter than mise,
I see what I see,
No one can see that the sky is so blue

Poetry Inspired by Van Gogh's "Starry Night"

Reborn

By Leila Goldstein

I was standing on the street one day, looking at the cars passing by. When I looked at one of the cars, it looked like the cute face of an animal. Suddenly I realized it was heading straight toward me! Why was it doing this? I realized that in a couple of seconds I would be dead. I froze. Then I died.

I am a girl, and my name is Alex. You might have noticed that in most stories, I would be dead and the story would end. But not this one; in this one this is the beginning.

I woke up in a very boring white room. I was on the floor and there wasn't any furniture. The floor was more white than white, and the walls were the same. There weren't any doors, so I was trapped.

Suddenly, somebody appeared in front of me. I stood up faster than lightning. The woman in front of me wasn't some evil death person or someone that matched the room with white clothes--it was a normal person, wearing a red shirt that said "Corllor Academy for Murdered Kids." Wait, that wasn't normal! Why did this women's shirt say that? Why would you want your shirt to say "murdered kids" on it?

"Hello," she said.

"Where…where am I?" I asked.

"Corllor Academy. I will explain everything on the way." she said.

"What? Where are you taking me?" I asked.

"You can't go on to the afterlife without getting full education. I'm taking you to your dorm and to the main school where you can continue your education until you're an adult," she said, as she handed me a binder.

"What's this?" I asked.

"You ask a lot of questions," she said. "It is the rules. I am Miss Chester. I will show you your schedule soon, but first we must get going."

My head was swimming with questions, but I didn't want her to get mad so I just kept my mouth shut.

"Here," said Miss Chester. She handed me a bracelet. "Put it on." I slipped the bracelet onto my wrist.

"What is it?" I asked.

Lunch When Your Parents Won't Make Food
By: Luna Rose Randolph

Ingredients:
1. Bread
2. Tomato sauce
3. Cheese
4. Pepperoni
5. Knife
6. Plate

Instructions:
1. First you get all your ingredients
2. After that you spread your tomato sauce on your bread.
3. Then you sprinkle cheese on the tomato sauce.
4. After that you can put on pepperoni. (This is optional)
5. Then you put it in the microwave and set the microwave to 1 minutes.
6. Enjoy!

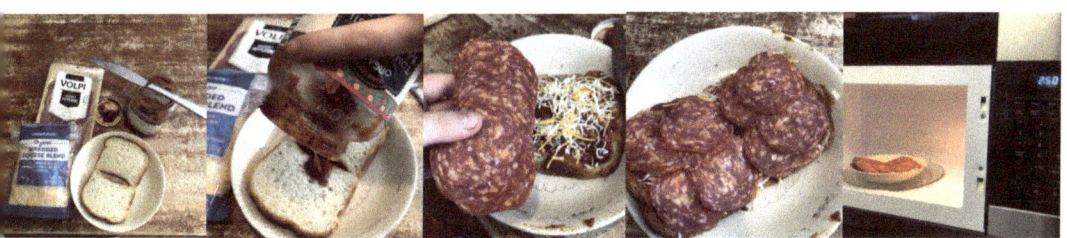

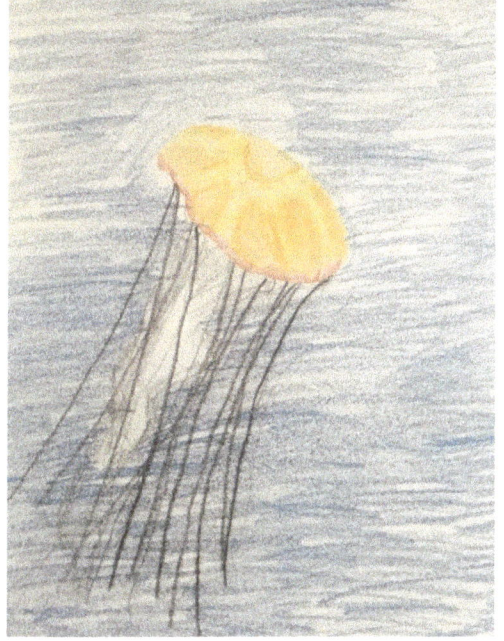

"Jellyfish" Art by Leila

Hello, my fellow sea cucumbers. This is the ***Super Pooper Story***. If you want to add something, you must put in your name, and only add something less than four sentences. You must also wait until a few more people have gone after you before you go again. I shall start it.

Matty: Once upon a time, Eric the dwarf was climbing on his roof when…

James: he fell off. Then he broke his…leg. And when he did, he screamed:

Luna: "I NEVER WANTED TO BE ALIVE!" as his underwear fell off.

Crispin: Meanwhile, Bobby mcStarsquish was tap-dancing on a sponge. The reason he was tap- dancing on a sponge was:

Annika: Because his floor was very dirty, so he thought he'd do two things at once. But…

Leila: he didn't have any soap so it wasn't working, and his floor was…

Crispin: turning into soup! Suddenly, he fell into his basement, which happened to be full of…

Luna: Cow poop.

Matty: And it just so happened that this cow poop belonged to Eric the Dwarf, who came in at that very moment and said:

Crispin: That's my cow poop, go get your own, ya little:

Leila: poop stealer, WHAT ARE YOU TRYING TO DO:

Crispin: TO MY POOP!?!?!?! AND WHAT ON EARTH ARE YOU DOING WITH THAT SPONGE?!?!?!? I'M SO MAD I'M GOING TO….

Luna: Poop on YOU THAT SHOULD TEACH YOU A LESSON AND AFTER I POOP ON YOU I AM GOING TO…

Matty: But Eric wasn't able to finish, because at that moment, a giant vortex opened up and it sent Eric and Bobby to….

Crispin: Stinkyland, the amusement park made entirely out of rotten eggs! The smell was so strong that Eric instantly…

Ava: Fell onto a roller coaster of poop and the handle was made out of…

Leila: hard rotten eggs with glue for extra:

Crispin: smelliness.

Matty: But the roller coaster went off course, flying off the tracks and into a…

Luna: Graveyard, and then

Crispin: they landed in the Zombie Ice Cream Man's cart. Suddenly, a container of Mint Chocolate Brains spilled, causing Eric to...

Matty: Break out in hives. He ran around screaming and eventually fell into a pit of gooey black

Ava: Fungus! And then he broke out into even more hives and his face puffed out like a red balloon.

Tracy: What a day!

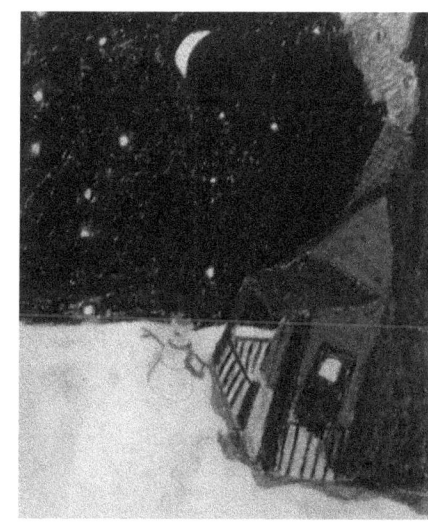

Art "Snowy House" by Leila

Ava's Sweet Sourdough Farm Bread

By: Ava Muhlestein

Ingredients:

- 1 ½ cups of warm water
- 2 cups of active yeast starter
- 5 cups of flour
- ¼ cup of brown sugar
- 1 TB Salt
- 2 TB White Sugar
- ½ cup of Raisins
- 2 TB of vegetable oil

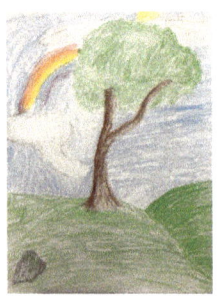

-Makes two loaves of bread
-If not making sweet bread, leave out brown sugar and raisins.

1- Combine Warm Water, Yeast Starter (not dry yeast), White Sugar and Salt into a bowl, and mix.
2- Add Flour, Brown Sugar, and Raisins Mix with a fork vigorously, make sure you combine all the ingredients.Place plastic wrap over bowl and place bowl into the refrigerator, let sit overnight, eight hours, or until dough has doubled in size..
3- Pour 1TB of oil into each loaf pan (two loaf pans), and remove the bowl from the refrigerator. and divide dough into two loaves and carefully pour dough into loaf pans, making sure there is equal dough in each pan.
4- Let rise for 4 hours or until the dough has doubled in size again.
5- Preheat the oven to 450, and place a pan full of water in the oven to add steam and so the bread will cook evenly.
6- Cook bread for 25 minutes or until bread is golden brown
7- Wait for bread to cool and enjoy with lots of butter!

"Lake" and "Tree on a Hill" Drawings by Leila

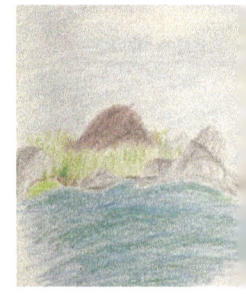

TRACY'S UPCOMING CLASSES 2021

WINTER: JANUARY-MARCH 2021

Mondays: We Make the World Magazine Issue 3: *Hibernating Dreamland*
Tuesdays: Teen Writer's Toolshed Session 1: *Choose Your Own Adventure*
Wednesdays: Young Writers Lab: *A Grimm Adaptation*
Fridays: Armenian Mythology Movie Makers

SPRING: APRIL-JUNE 2021

Mondays: We Make the World Magazine Issue 4: *Blooming Heart Beginnings*
Tuesdays: Teen Writer's Toolshed Session 2: *A Hero's Journey*
Wednesdays: Young Writers Lab: *Otherworlds*
Fridays: Celtic Mythology Movie Makers

SUMMER: JULY-AUGUST 2021

- Young Writers Magazine Lab:
  We Make the World Magazine Issue 5
  "We Are Wild Things" (July-August TBD)

- Young Anthology Project w/ Camp NaNoWriMo (July TBD)

- Stop Motion Makers - Gnomes & Fairies (TBD)

- A Grimm Movie Makers (TBD)

FALL: SEPTEMBER-NOVEMBER 2021

Mondays: Teen Writers Toolshed: Who Dun It? A Mystery! (Sep-Oct)
Tuesdays: We Make the World Magazine Issue 6: "Letting Go"
Wednesdays: Young Writers Lab: Spooktacular Short Stories (Sep-Oct)
Fridays: Japanese Mythology & Yokai Movie Makers

Mondays & Wednesdays in November: Young Author Intensive
                                        NaNoWriMo 2021

==Winter, Spring, & Fall Sessions==

The Teen Writers Toolshed:

How to Build Stories That Matter

Ages 12-15

Classes on ZOOM

==THREE 12 WEEK SESSIONS with PODCAST extension!==

==Winter Session 1:==	*Spring Session 2:*	==Fall Session 3:==
January 5th-March 23rd	April 6th-June 22nd	*Sept. 6th-Oct. 25th
Tuesdays 4-6pm	Tuesdays 4-6pm	Mondays 4-6pm

Students will activate their imaginations and inspire one another in this collaborative forum to create original work. Writers will delight in activities that create a safe container for their ideas to manifest. Our group of creators will receive positive and constructive feedback to perfect and evolve their stories, all while gaining various tools to construct their ideas clearly. Students will enjoy having creative writing challenges, dedicated time for free and focused writing, collaborative brainstorming, and the needed accountability to set and reach goals. Leaders that are interested in shaping a new podcast, will work with Tracy to form an audio extension to this class!

Young Writers will create a special collaborative anthology of their best work as a keepsake!

Artistic Director, Tracy Randolph and Children's Author, Geneva Clawson, will challenge and inspire students to find their voice and create stories that excite and matter to them!

COST: **$625** (Per 12 week Session) *8week Fall Cost TBD

Optional Student Led Zoom "Coworking" project hours - Saturdays 2-4pm

TO ENROLL: Tracy at (925) 822-5435 OR

tracyrandolph@hotmail.com

COMING THIS WINTER!!!

World Mythology Movie Makers:
Armenian History, Folktales, & Fables

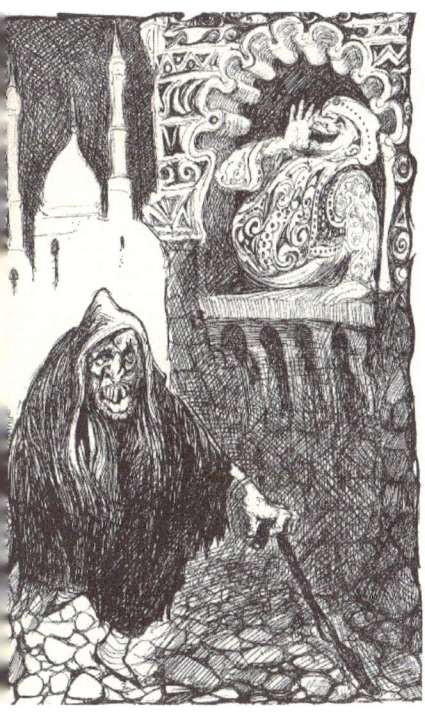

January 8th - March 26th:
*Fridays from 10-1pm

Let's travel to the Ancient land of Armenia. We will celebrate Armenia's rich culture, colorful folktales & mythology, and historical story of struggle and survival. From pagan roots through Christianity, students will learn about the genocide, current politics, and ultimately work on a large group Movie Maker film production that culminates what they have learned and focuses on a favorite fable or myth. Students will

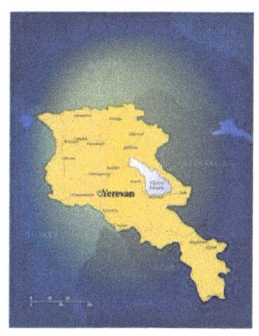

synthesize what they have learned into a student produced final script and have the opportunity to audition for a role, create original artwork, learn about acting through ensemble work and voice-over production, and experience a film production like no other! Students and families will celebrate all the hard work by viewing the finished film once it's edited, after the series ends, at a special family potluck movie premiere celebration!

COST $625

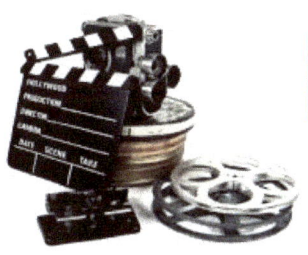
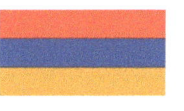

*with a 20 minute lunch break

Geared for ages 8-14

TO ENROLL: Contact Tracy Randolph @ (925) 822-5435 or tracyrandolph@hotmail.com

*Optional Student Led Zoom "Co-Working" project hours on Saturdays 2-4pm

YOUNG WRITERS MAGAZINE LAB

"WE MAKE THE WORLD MAGAZINE"

Literary & Art classes on ZOOM
Ages 8-14

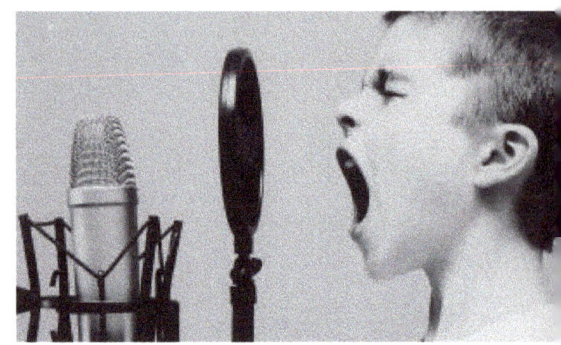

==12 WEEK SESSION:==

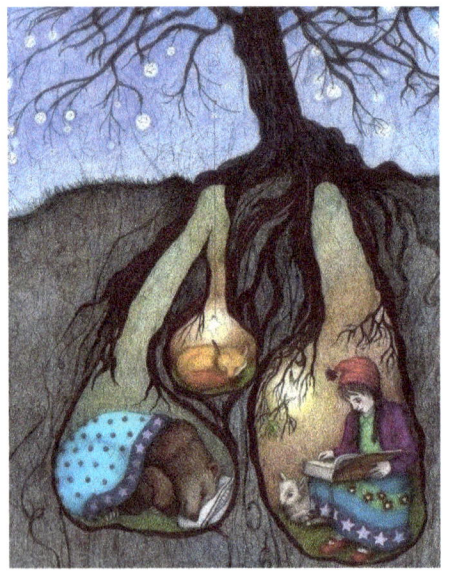

Winter Session 1 Intensive:
"Hibernating Dreamland"
January 4th-March 22nd 2021
Mondays from 4-6pm

Have you ever wanted to write a story? Poetry? Your thoughts about life, the world, your observations? Can you imagine picking up a magazine that you've written? The kind of magazine that was written by people your age, with you in mind? In this *Young Writers Lab* students will have the time, inspiration, and accountability within an artistic community of fellow young writers to create and self publish a collaborative magazine written by and for young people called "We Make the World". Students will work together to weave a series of essays, interviews, short scripts, stories, poetry, thoughts, artwork, and other inspirations. Let's take our creativity to the next level!

COST $625

- Students will need to come to class prepared with paper, pencils, colors, and access to a digital camera or smartphone, GoogleDocs, and a device to email photographed artwork.
- One copy of Fall Issue #2 with enrollment - extra copies at additional cost

CONTACT Tracy at (925) 822-5435 or at tracyrandolph@hotmail.com

Optional Student Led Zoom "Co-Working" project hours on Saturdays 2-4pm

Young Writers Lab:
A Grimm Adaptation

January 6th - March 24th
Wednesdays 4-6pm

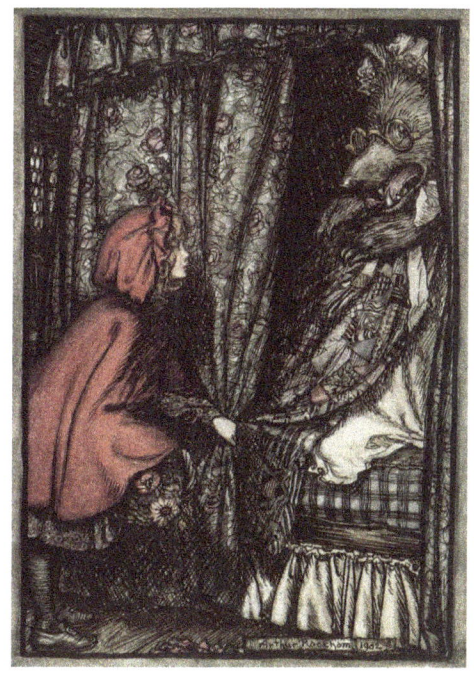

A poor man. A son. A girl. A mother. A king and a queen. Twelve brothers. The Grimm stories are about all kinds of people. From peasants to kings. From murderers to priests. Not to mention imaginative creatures like giants, elves, and water nixies.

In fairy tales, there are few limits on who we can create or the stories we tell. Our characters don't necessarily have to look or act a certain way. A young woman can have impossibly long hair, or a man can turn into a lion during the day. And an innocent looking spindle can change the course of a kingdom's history. Students will do a deep dive into how the Grimms handle key elements of genre, character, setting, plot, fairy tale magic, and theme as we adapt the original stories into reimagined ones of our own!

Many of the fairy tales we are familiar with today have gone through a number of changes to become more kid-friendly, and audiences might be surprised to read the often cruel and disturbing endings of the Grimms' original tales. For example, did you know that in the Grimms' tale of Snow White, the wicked queen is punished at the end of the story and made to dance to her death wearing a pair of red hot iron shoes? (Pretty *grim*, right?)

Join us for 12 weeks of storytelling, reimaging, and adapting these classic folklore tales into our own Grim Tales! Students will work together to adapt these tales and artwork to go with them in a final Grim Anthology!

COST $625

- Students will need to come to class prepared with a journal, art supplies & access to email and GoogleDocs

CONTACT Tracy at (925) 822-5435 or at tracyrandolph@hotmail.com

Optional Student Led Zoom "Co-Working" project hours on Saturdays 2-4pm

COMING THIS SPRING!!!

World Mythology Movie Makers:
CELTIC MYTHOLOGY

April 9th – June 25th:
*Fridays from 10-1pm

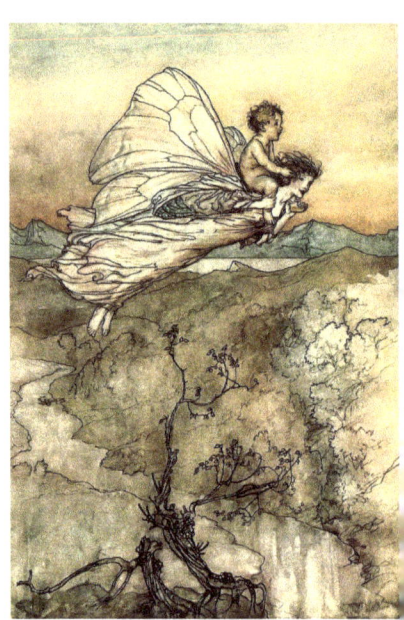

Come unlock the magical realm of Gnomes, Faeries, Banshees, Changelings and many more wondrous creatures that inhabit the ancient Celtic story world.

Students will work on a large group Movie Maker film production that culminates what they have learned and focuses on a favorite fable, myth, or bit of lore. Students will synthesize what they have learned into a student produced final script and have the opportunity to audition for a role, create original artwork, learn about acting through ensemble work and voice-over production, and experience a film production like no other! Students and families will celebrate all the hard work by viewing the finished film once it's edited, after the series ends, at a special family potluck movie premiere celebration!

COST $625

*with a 20 minute lunch break

Geared for ages 8-14

TO ENROLL: (925) 822-5435 or
tracyrandolph@hotmail.com

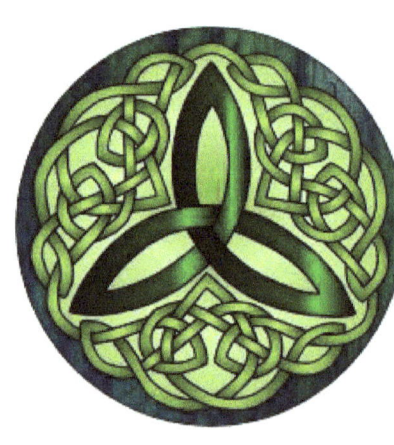

*Optional Student Led Zoom "Co-Working" project hours on Saturdays 2-4pm

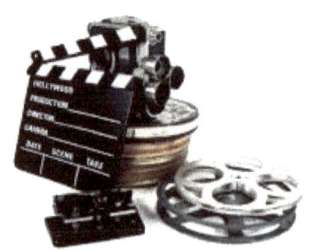

YOUNG WRITERS MAGAZINE LAB

"WE MAKE THE WORLD MAGAZINE"

Literary & Art classes on ZOOM
Ages 8-14

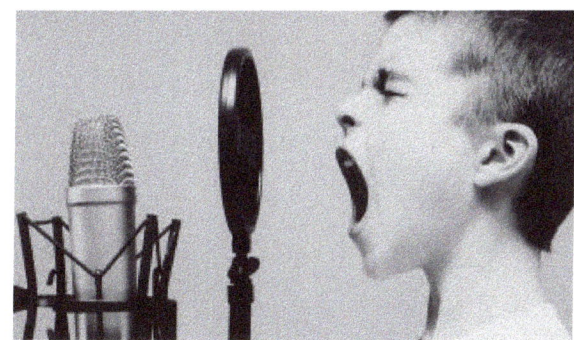

12 WEEK SESSION:

Spring Session 2 Intensive: "Blooming Heart"
April 5th-June 21st 2021
Mondays from 4-6pm

Have you ever wanted to write a story? Poetry? Your thoughts about life, the world, your observations? Can you imagine picking up a magazine that you've written? The kind of magazine that was written by people your age, with you in mind? In this *Young Writers Lab* students will have the time, inspiration, and accountability within an artistic community of fellow young writers to create and self publish a collaborative magazine written by and for young people called "We Make the World". Students will work together to weave a series of essays, interviews, short scripts, stories, poetry, thoughts, artwork, and other inspirations. Let's take our creativity to the next level!

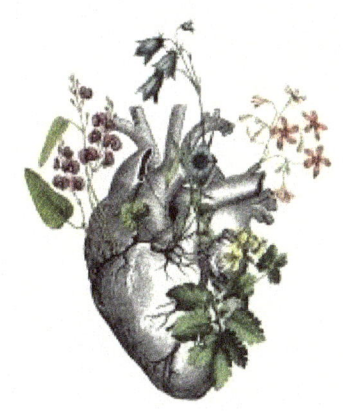

COST $625

- Students will need to come to class prepared with paper, pencils, colors, and access to a digital camera or smartphone, GoogleDocs, and a device to email photographed artwork.
- One copy of Fall Issue #2 with enrollment - extra copies at additional cost

CONTACT Tracy at (925) 822-5435 or at tracyrandolph@hotmail.com

*Optional Student Led Zoom "Co-Working" project hours on Saturdays 2-4pm

Young Writer Lab: *Otherworlds*

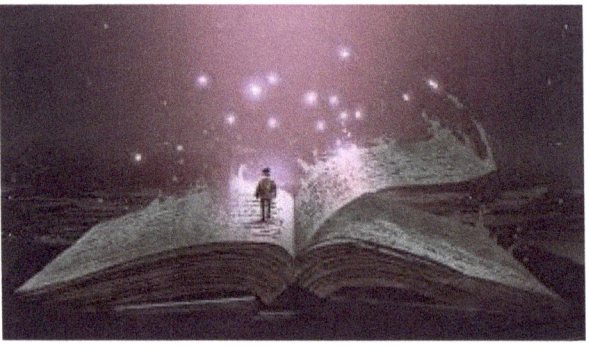

April 7th - June 23rd 2021 ~ Wednesdays 4-6pm

Join us on our world mythology adventure as we veer off our known mortal world. Leap into the unknown realm of the knowledge keepers and play God/Goddess to create your own dynamic/symbolic/metaphorical mythologies in story form.

Students will access the teachings of Joseph Campbell and join the likes of other epic story creators like George Lucas and J.K. Rowling! Young Writers will invent new worlds, stories, myths, and legends of their own. We will pay attention to primal archetypes, symbology, and universal forces as we attempt to give meaning and purpose to life's big questions, lighting the eternal flame of curiosity wrapped up in our own mysterious stories.

Students will collaborate in a final *Otherworld Adventure Anthology* with potential for publication. Although the focus of this class is on writing, students will be encouraged to access their own artistic tools of expression to bring their creations to life visually as well.

COST $625

- Students will need to come to class prepared with a journal, art supplies & access to email and GoogleDocs

CONTACT Tracy at (925) 822-5435 or at tracyrandolph@hotmail.com
*Optional Student Led Zoom "Co-Working" project hours on Saturdays 2-4pm

COMING THIS FALL!!!

World Mythology Movie Makers:

JAPANESE YOKAI

September 10th - November 26th:
*Fridays from 10-1pm

Come explore into Japanese supernatural Yokai folklore this Fall!

In ancient Japan, spirits were thought to be formless and invisible to the human eye.

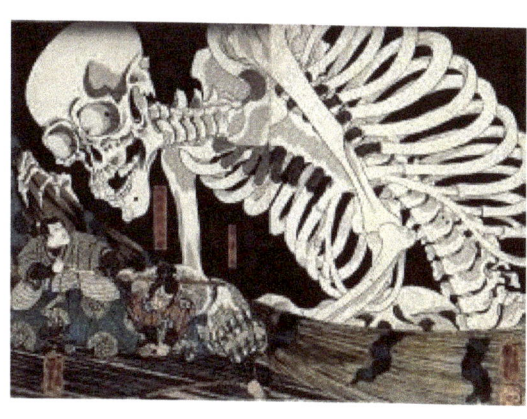

However, as artistic traditions developed, it became necessary to visually depict the spirits and monsters from stories. During the Edo period (1603-1868), there was an unprecedented flourishing of culture and art in Japan. Ghost stories and stories about monsters and strange phenomena from all over Japan experienced a huge surge in popularity.

Today, the influence of yōkai can again be seen in all aspects of Japanese culture, from manga and anime, to video games, brand labels, and even on Japanese currency.

Students will work on a large group Movie Maker film production that culminates what they have learned and focuses on a favorite fable, myth, Yokai or bit of lore. Students will synthesize what they have learned into a student produced final script and have the opportunity to audition for a role, create original artwork, learn about acting through ensemble work and voice-over production, and experience a film production like no other! Students and families will celebrate all the hard work by viewing the finished film once it's edited, after the series ends, at a special family potluck movie premiere celebration!

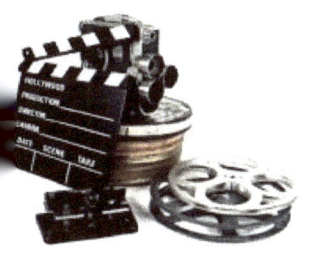

COST $625

*with a 20 minute lunch break

Geared for ages 8-14

TO ENROLL: (925) 822-5435 or
tracyrandolph@hotmail.com

*Optional Student Led Zoom "Co-Working" project hours on Saturdays 2-4pm

YOUNG WRITERS MAGAZINE LAB

"WE MAKE THE WORLD MAGAZINE"

Literary & Art classes on ZOOM
Ages 8-14

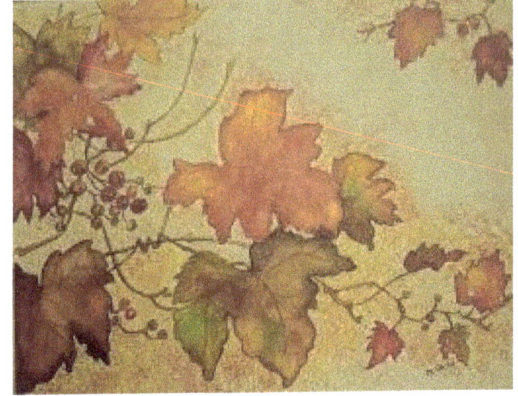

12 WEEK SESSION:

Fall Session 4 Intensive:
"Letting Go"
September-November 2021
Tuesdays from 4-6pm

Have you ever wanted to write a story? Poetry? Your thoughts about life, the world, your observations? Can you imagine picking up a magazine that you've written? The kind of magazine that was written by people your age, with you in mind? In this *Young Writers Lab* students will have the time, inspiration, and accountability within an artistic community of fellow young writers to create and self publish a collaborative magazine written by and for young people called "We Make the World". Students will work together to weave a series of essays, interviews, short scripts, stories, poetry, thoughts, artwork, and other inspirations. Let's take our creativity to the next level!

COST $625

- Students will need to come to class prepared with paper, pencils, colors, and access to a digital camera or smartphone, GoogleDocs, and a device to email photographed artwork.
- One copy of Fall Issue #2 with enrollment - extra copies at additional cost

CONTACT Tracy at (925) 822-5435 or at tracyrandolph@hotmail.com

Optional Student Led Zoom "Co-Working" project hours on Saturdays 2-4pm

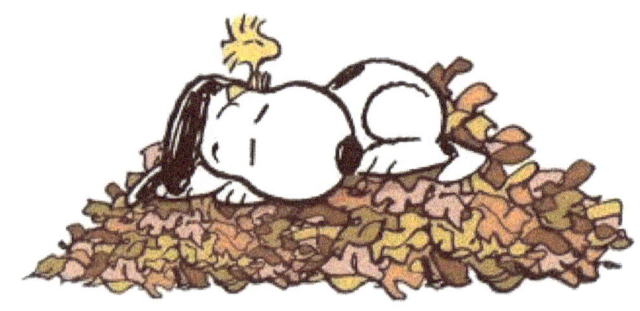

Here's what parents and students are saying about Tracy's classes:

"Annika loves 'Miss Tracy'. As a mom, to be a fly on the wall during Tracy's classes is a magical thing. She brings a deep understanding of how children learn, and invites each child into a safe, supportive space in which their own, unique voice is heard and honored. Tracy and the kids truly form a community. The meld of history, culture, art, and movie making is brilliant—so many ways to learn, process, and express subjects and themes, all while receiving a gentle introduction to life skills around collaboration, goal setting, and accountability." -**Dawn (Mom)**

"I like that she's very generous and gives us a lot of chances to make our work better. She mentors us so well and helps us through things." –James (student)

"Teacher Tracy is the best! We have enjoyed her classes for the last two years. She is patient with the kids and really cares about them individually. We appreciate her generous nature and willingness to share her knowledge and skills". -**Dana (Mom)**

"I really like how she's kind and supportive and gives me good ideas. She's very motivational and she leaves a lot of things open ended so we can make it our own." - **Crispin (student)**

"I think your teaching style is amazing. It's such a warm atmosphere, even online. I love how you let the kids have brainstorming time but it's almost like a guided meditation, where your voice comes in occasionally to keep them thinking freely and reminding them not to erase or criticize what they just wrote. I also appreciate how you keep them positive but specific and honest in helping each other be better writers. You make them feel safe and inspired to express what's inside themselves. Now I understand how INSPIRED they have been this week to just keep writing. Thank you for inspiring our kids to be their most self-expressive, creative selves! - **Vanitha (Mom)**

"Tracy's classes give me a lot of creative freedom to write whatever I feel like! She also frequently gives feedback to work which is great! She is always supportive of what we're writing and is a great teacher and her classes helped me a lot in developing my writing skills." – **Judah (student)**

"Tracy's classes are amazing! She is passionate about what she does and innovative in how she does it. The kids are able to learn about subjects while at the same time watch their own visions come to life...there is no better education model. To stir imagination and curiosity, educate and inspire, then create! Hands on learning. Tracys is open, supportive and kind, we are lucky to have her as a teacher in our daughter's life! I cannot recommend her classes enough!!"
- **George (Dad)**

"Ms. Tracy is extraordinary! The camps she teaches are all kinds of awesome and very unique. They cover really interesting topics, and she gives us great feedback on what we can do to improve. She also has these 'daily quotes' that help us take our writing to the next level. If I could choose any summer camp, it would be Ms. Tracy's." -**Raini (student)**

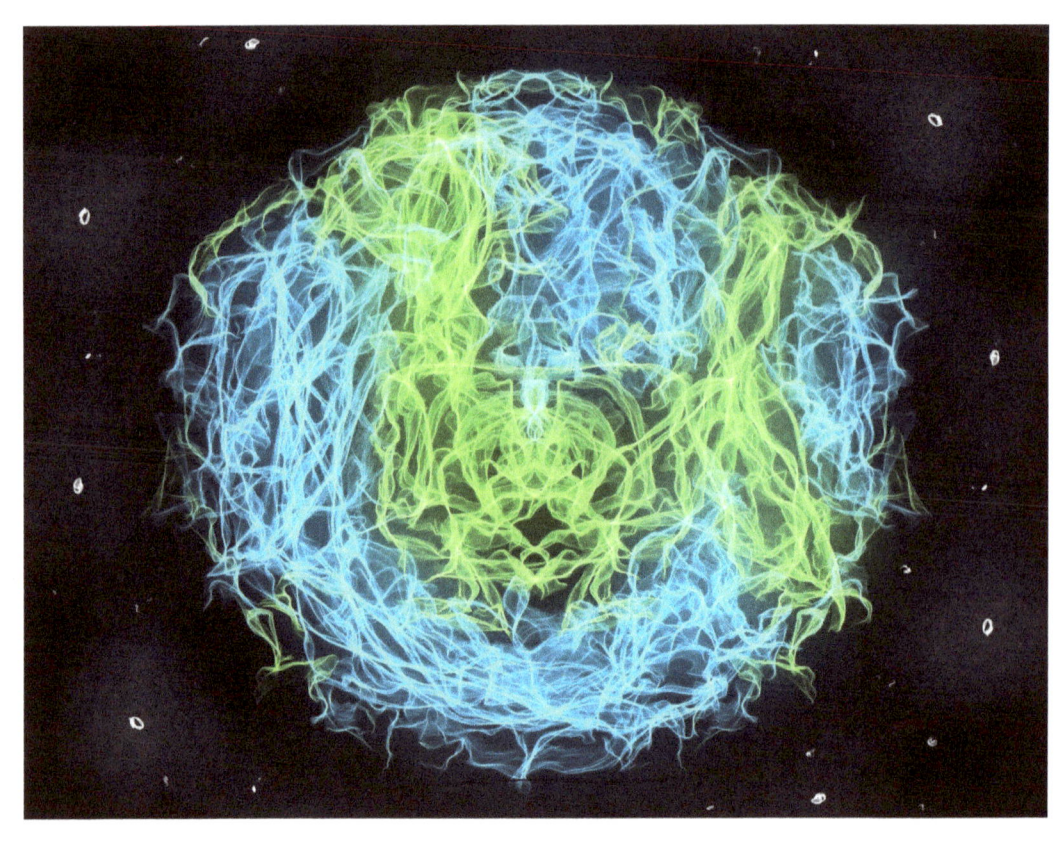

"Everyone thinks of changing the world, but no one thinks of changing himself."

— Leo Tolstoy

www.ingramcontent.com/pod-product-compliance
Lightning Source LLC
Chambersburg PA
CBHW040522220526
45473CB00013B/2955